# Horsemanship

Equine Communication

The Mind Connection

Holly Davis

Copyright © 2014 Holly Davis

All Rights Reserved.

ISBN-10: 1507839316
ISBN-13: 978-1507839317

This book may not be reproduced in whole or part in any form or by any means, electronic, mechanical, or otherwise without permission from the Author. Except by a reviewer, who may quote brief paragraphs in a review.

For all other permissions, please contact the Author

www.hollydavis.co.uk

## DEDICATION

For all horses…
From those I call my own, as well as all horses that have ventured into the world of humans

May your voices all be heard

# ACKNOWLEDGEMENTS

## Photographs

Susan and Tim Duckworth at Bitless and Barefoot

Madara Enkuzena

## Original Cover Photograph

Gordon Patterson
www.gordonpattersonphotography.co.uk

# CONTENTS

Introduction..................................................9

1. What is Horse Communication?......................21
2. Clearing Negative Thought Patterns..........26
3. Meditation................................................37
4. How We Receive Information..................43
5. The Horse & Human Connection.............48
6. What Horses Know...................................56
7. How to Interpret.......................................73
8. Conducting a Session...............................80
9. Body Scanning.........................................97
10. Earth Energies........................................107
11. Working with Other Therapists...............112
12. What are We Really Telling Them?.................128
13. Ethics and Legalities..............................133
14. Tracking Lost and Stolen Animals............139
15. Choose Your Title Carefully...................148
16. Are Horses Psychic or Intuitive?...................155
17. Why Ask for Questions..........................160
18. Assessing Pain Levels............................162
19. The Fine Line of Diagnosing..................166
20. The Selective Communicator..................174
21. Autism, Learning Difficulties and Dementia 177
22. The Psychological Safety Zone...............183
23. Save Them All Syndrome.....................190
24. Looking Glass Syndrome.......................200
25. Sympathy vs Empathy...........................206

About the Author.......................................211

# INTRODUCTION

*Sometimes horse whispers....*

*Sometimes horse screams....*

Just how he is heard, and if he is heard, is down to each and every one of us. It is our responsibility to enable him to have his voice, and enable his voice to be heard.

*We must not let him suffer in silence*

Back in 1999 when I began teaching Animal Communication, it was a subject that a few knew about and had heard of, but it was far from being mainstream and as much known of as it is today. If you were to ask the average horse person now if they had heard of Horse Communication, it is likely that the majority will have. Though due to a lack of knowledge and all too often fear - many will have avoided it or are sceptical - but hey that is OK!

Horse Communication is a very personal thing and in many ways a personal belief. Whether someone chooses to believe in it or not, may even beyond their control. However, a belief in Horse Communication is not a perquisite for its existence - it will not cease to exist just because someone does not think it possible. The horses have so much they need to say and so much they need us to know. By going into our hearts and enabling that true connection of mind to mind and heart to heart - they can and will be heard.

I have been teaching Horse Communication and working with clients all over the word for sixteen years now. Not a day goes by that I am not humbled by the information that comes from horses. Their carefully chosen words, their unique personalities and opinions, as well as their kindness and lack of judgment towards the humans that so often abuse and forsake them.

Literally thousands of conversations later I am still

learning from my horse friends. Both those I call my own, and those that live with friends and clients. With each communication comes new information and new insights: the horse in pain, the joyful horse and the horse whose 'time' has come. Their personalities are as diverse as are found in the human world. There is one thing that I can never stress enough - that is that we must never stop listening and we must never stop learning. The horses need us - they need us to hear them, help them, help ourselves and create change in the world of equestrianism that is so sadly letting down, crippling and destroying so many of our horse friends.

But there is good news too. That good news is that 'you' can hear them if you allow; you can help them, and you too can help create change in the horse world. For each horse we help, the ripples are sent out - word spreads and more horses are helped. Be one who is not afraid to throw the pebble and create those ripples that will spread far and wide - do it for the horses, and do it for yourself. I assure you - you will find your fulfillment and your vocation within this sacred connection that is the horse.

Even if your interest lies just with your own horse's and the need and desire to connect with them on a deeper level. Then I have no doubt the following chapters will help you to explore the world of Horse Communication in a way that will help you to achieve this connection. This book equally is for those that wish to work on a higher level and gain a direct connection with all horses that they encounter. In order to give them a voice and help to create change both for the horses themselves - and those that have an open heart and mind that they live with.

Horse Communication is as easy or as hard as you allow and enable it to be.

We all have the ability to hear horses. All too often it is our lack of knowledge and our fear that stops us. However, this can be overcome if there is a heart-felt desire within you, and in wanting a clear and free dialogue to happen. There are no limitations to what can be asked; it is no different to how we would openly sit and listen to another person talk or ask them questions. Horses, like people, all have their own unique personalities that makes them both who and how they are. Some will be open and chatty, whilst some may hold back a little until they feel they are comfortable with you. How you approach each horse mentally and how you are feeling at that time, plays a huge role on the outcome. However, just because we ask a question it does not ultimately mean that the horse has to, or even wants to answer - they may not even be able to. All too often it is within the wording and phasing of the question and how we mentally and emotionally approach the horse, that is the deciding factor in how easily the answer is offered by them, and heard by us.

The biggest hurdle that we may come across besides our own fear, is our level and lack of equine knowledge. Due to the way in which Horse Communication works, we can only repeat the words that we know and can understand, as well as our ability to repeat and explain what the horse says. As in order to do this, we need to understand the subject matter to enable us to form it into words.

But horses don't speak in words and English many will cry! Yes, that's right they don't - but that does not mean that they are not heard in words, due to the complexity and yet easy to fathom human mind when we put it to good use. We need to learn to be open and willing to accept all that we hear from horses and all that they have to offer. No matter how hard that is to bare sometimes.

By denying a horse his voice and only hearing him selectively, due to our own fear of what we may hear – we are not working with our true integrity. The horse will know this - he will feel it from us even if our words do not convey it. For this reason it is of utmost importance that we be open within ourselves in regards to our intention, and that we do not lie to ourselves as to how we feel and our true intent.

Horse Communication is not for everyone; some may 'hear' but it is just not for them. For some people in their early days, what may be heard can feel sad - even shocking. We may take those feelings to bed with us and they may keep us awake at night. This is why within these chapters I will also be gently guiding you through some observations that I have made and explaining them to you. In the hope that they will enable you to see another side to things and in how you feel and are able to control those emotions. By doing this, Horse Communication, your ability to hear and not fear - will come easily for you. You will simply allow the dialogue to flow with no fear over what will be heard. The true art of being a Horse Communicator in this mind to mind connective way, is in being able to master the 'this is about the horse, it is not about me'. The horse may not 'like' where he is and 'how' his life is - but on some level he will have chosen it, and there is a reason for him being there and him going through what he is.

It maybe that he needs to be with that certain owner

(For the purpose of this book I will use the term 'owner'. However, this no way implies that we can ever 'own' a horse in anyway shape or form. It is purely for ease of reference and to mean the person that has 'bought' the horse, or the person with which the horse lives - usually a care-giver) for whatever reason, or that one or both of them have a lesson to learn. Whatever the reason it still does not mean that there aren't things that can be changed for the better and aided and improved where needed. Without a life path or karma being affected.

Our role in Horse Communication is simply to be a tool that the horse can use in the way that he needs to in order that his voice can be heard - WITHOUT BIAS. We are of little use to the horse if we choose to block what we hear and unintentionally (likely subconsciously and unknowingly) put our own twist on it, as it then sits more comfortably with us to hear and repeat – as this is then not the full truth from the horse. It is not for us to decide 'how' the horse should be heard and is feeling, any more than it is for us to decide how life should be for him. Through his past months and years and his training and handling he will have formed a picture of how he knows life will suit him best. Although as with people - there will also be those that are a little confused as to their wants, needs and desires. Our role instead, is to hear what he has to say in its entirety - without judgment and prejudice, our role is to just simply be the go between and his voice.

Over the years there has been a fast and steady flow of new Horse Communicators emerging. Those that have been communicating for years that now only feel the time is right for them to speak up, and those that are new to this subject. As with any career there will be the good and the bad and those with good integrity and those lacking in it. For some it is simply a money spinner and a way of stroking their own ego. For others it becomes a way of life that quite literally spreads and flows into every aspect of their life - it just becomes 'who they are' rather than 'what they do' - a way of life - rather than just a career.

When we look at the Internet we see no end of websites advertising horse and animal communication services. Some that make the claim of being the world's leading, the UK's leading, America's leading and so on - this is of utmost arrogance in itself. These claims are made by those that have elected that title for themselves in order to sway people their way. It is not a title the horses have handed to them, any more than it is a title they are deserving of. With so many people developing at such a fast and productive rate, there will already be those that have exceeded those peoples abilities and all too often, their integrity also. How do these self-titled world class and world leading people know they are the 'best'? Further more: Why do they need to feel and make themselves out to be better than anyone else? Surely that is for the horses to decide? Besides which, somewhere out in the world a little man may be sitting in his log cabin in the woods spending his days communication with horses all over the world. Maybe he is changing lives as we speak? If he is - I doubt he has any desire to create his own glory and band it about through self-given titles in a bid to pull the wool over the eyes of others.

These Communicators have a desire to maintain their 'status', they are afraid that others will see through them, and God forbid get to the level of admiration they believe people hold for them. They do not want others to develop in the way they believe they have done. They do not want others to achieve that kind of (delusional) notoriety. To do so could earn them a title and status that has actually been earnt and offered by others, that would then override their own self elected one. They have no desire of that, they wish to remain at the top where they believe they deserve to be and think they are.

Who they are leading exactly? Dogs on leads? A flock of sheep? Whilst some experienced Horse Communicators may be able of offer guidance and knowledge to help you along your way. Your journey with horses is what it is - it is 'your' journey. It is not for those wishing to learn to have to, or feel the need to follow others, or put them on a pedestal. They are quite simply their own person with their own intellect and ability to work things out for themselves.

Horse Communication 'is' and always 'should' be about helping horses - not human elitism.

Not everyone wants to get on aeroplanes and fly to other countries to give seminars. Some people are just as happy working away quietly in the back ground, with horses and in peace. Some prefer to spend time with their horses and mutually enjoy in that quality time, rather than communicating publicly in front of 'adoring' audiences.

Instead, we must strive to be the best we can be as an individual. It is the horses after all that will decide who and what we are, when they connect with our offered energy we send out - whether we intend it or not. They are the ones who will decide - not us, only those titles offered by the horse are the ones that are deserved and do not even need to be spoken of.

Further to this, as Horse Communicators, our ability to communicate and clearly 'hear' the horse in a mind to mind connection, is also largely governed by the horses' own ability to clearly connect. In other words, we can only communicate as well as the horse with which we are communicating with.

As Horse Communicators we need to learn many lessons from the horse. One of those all too important lessons is to remain humble and not put ourselves on a pedestal. If we choose to do so the fall may be a long one with a nasty thump at the bottom. One which I have already seen some Horse Communicators meet with through no fault other than their own. Do not allow yourself to become one of those - maintain your integrity - remain humble. Be like the horse and he will recognise this within you.

Needless to say there are a huge amount of Horse Communicators out there that have a very limited knowledge of horses and the equestrian world in general. Sadly this will and does have an impact on how many of us that are not so limited are viewed by the general public. All too often when people discover their ability to hear horses, they rush out to quickly and begin to work professionally. This may be due to financial reasons, a desire to help horses, or because they feel they are ready. However, none of these are good enough reasons. It is not about the money - it is about helping horses. We can only help horses when we are knowledgeable enough, are integral and informed. Also, we need to truly be ready to venture out and not just think that we are. One of the first lessons in Horse Communication without a doubt, is to understand that the more we learn, the more likely we are to know just how much we don't know. That is the driving force that needs to be behind each and every one of us - it is that which drives us forwards in order to learn, experience and aid horses everywhere.

So with all of that out of the way it is time to start learning, start working on ourselves and start helping the horses of the world who need us.

*Remain humble, remain open and maintain your integrity - the horses need you.*

# WHAT IS HORSE COMMUNICATION?

Horse Communication is the ability to read the vibration frequencies that are held within the horses' electromagnetic energy field - often referred to as the 'Aura'.

Each thought, feeling and illness carries its own unique vibrational signature.

The ability to connect in this way and to hear horses talking, is often referred to as telepathy. In recent years there has been some confusion as many Communicators have chosen to call themselves Horse Whisperers. 'Whispering' refers to the art of reading the minute body signals that the horse gives off and communication on a physical level. Horse communication is very different as the connection is purely mind to mind - energy to energy.

There are several other different titles used by Horse Communicators including: Horse Psychic and Telepathic Horse Communicator, all of which essentially come down to the same thing.

We will be covering the importance of choosing your title carefully later in this book, due to the influence it can have on the Horse Communication world at large.

When we are reading the vibrational frequencies from the horse in relation to their physical and emotional information. Our subconscious takes that information in and stores it whilst translating it into words, pictures and feelings. This information is then transferred to our conscious self in a way that we can understand. It is down to the individual Communicator as to exactly how this information is received. Some Communicators will 'feel' the information or physical ailments from the horse, some will see only pictures, and some will only hear the information through words. Most of us will receive the information through a collection of these to varying degrees. Many Horse Communicators never hear words being spoken, but the feelings and pictures are very strong, so their information is just as clear as if they were hearing the horse speak using actual words.

Often when a horse has a problem it can be viewing

things from a negative perspective, or not be able to see the bigger picture. Through communication we can talk to and council the horse in exactly the same way as we would a person. Sometimes just this alone is enough to break a cycle of unwanted behaviour by opening them up to a new perspective or understanding. Some animals just benefit from knowing that someone – you - are willing to listen and is there for them.

**Shamanic Horse Communication**

Shamanic Horse Communication is slightly different to mainstream Horse Communication, as when working with a horse in this way, we work with the help of a compassionate animal spirit. The term Shaman (referring to the person who practices shamanism) comes from Siberia, Tuva and Mongolia and is used to describe the person who practices the art of working with Animal Guides and venturing into the unseen realms. This often includes both guidance from the Animal Guides, as well as them passing on information relating physical health, healing and how any problems may be addressed. Therefore, Shamans are typically seen as Medicine Men. Shamanism is used extensively by the indigenous people, as well as many folk cultures all over the world.

It is now more commonly used by Horse Communicators than it has been in the past as is the knowledge and insight gained through it.

## Transpersonal Interspecies Communication

This is the ability to communicate will all living things and their energy fields. By this I mean everything and anything living. Everything living has an electromagnetic energy field. This means that they have the ability to store information within their field that we can read. When we are communicating with this 'part' of the living being, what we are actually communicating with, is a higher consciousness/part of their intelligence.

Transpersonal in simple terms could be interpreted as 'trans' - meaning in transit and 'personal' - as in personal to that individual.

This leaves us with a very good description of this part of the consciousness, as this part is often in transit, not being connected directly to the physical. It is a form of energy, as indeed all consciousness is. It has the ability to move in and out of the physical body and to be sent to all corners of the universe, in order to gain knowledge and information.

The transpersonal self is often referred to as the 'higher-self' or 'over-soul'.

## Transmigration

The migration or leaving of this part of the consciousness (in transit) that often involves the moving into, or attachment to, another physical body.

## Trans-Integration

The integration of this aspect of the consciousness that has attached to the physical body. Also, to the energy systems of the individual and in choosing to work with and through them.

# CLEARING NEGATIVE THOUGHT PATTERNS

Many of us have self-doubt associated with our ability to communicate with horses. Sometimes this will have come through lack of confidence or low self-esteem. If we are having problems communicating then we first need to analyse the reasons behind it. As much as many people want to communicate with horses, some may also have an underlying fear of what they may hear. When communicating with our own horses we have a deeper emotional connection. When we are worried and concerned about them, we can subconsciously block what it is we are hearing from them as a way of safe-guarding ourselves and our own emotions. Whilst this can sometimes appear helpful, it is really only blocking what we really need to hear in order to help both ourselves and our horses. By acknowledging our fear and seeing beyond it, we open ourselves up more widely to hearing what it is we truly need to hear. Many people experience the same kind of problems when trying to communicate with wild horses and those horses living with other people.

There can be many different reasons for why this is, but often the underlying factor is fear and discomfort. Many of us grow up being conditioned to believe in certain things. The problem being that when we choose to believe in one thing it can open up a whole chain of other beliefs being questioned.

Since communicating with horses may be the first link in this chain, we may block our abilities we have for communicating for fear of opening up a whole can of worms. Once we find ourselves communicating we are open to hearing things that challenge those beliefs and make us question everything we had trusted and learned up until this time.

## Examples

*Your horse trying to tell you that they are ready to die*

*Your horse telling you they are very ill*
*Your horse telling you that they no longer want to live with*

## The Chatterbox

Many of you would have experienced what I refer to as the 'chatterbox'. This is the self-destructive part of us. The part of us that tells us 'we aren't good enough' and repeatedly tells us 'no you can't do that', or 'no you're wrong, you can't possibly be hearing correctly'. I'm sure many of you will be able to relate to this and will have experienced it at some point. The subconscious part of our minds is very easily fooled and is subservient to our conscious mind. That is to say that if we are told something often or repeatedly enough, we think negatively about ourselves. We will in time convince ourselves that it is indeed true as our subconscious will come to believe it.

The important thing to remember is that as the chatterbox is part of our make-up, we will never be able to rid ourselves of it, only lessen it. The best way that this can be achieved is to firstly recognise when it is our chatterbox speaking, rather than our authentic self. So everything your mind tells you about yourself that is negative or upsetting in anyway it should be dismissed, as it is your chatterbox speaking. Every time you hear this voice replace the negative with a positive.

## Chatterbox

'I'm mad! Of course I can't hear horses speaking only special people can'!

## The True You

' I know I have the ability to hear horses speaking. The human and animal kingdoms are connected so that I can do this willingly and with ease'.

Once we start to fight back at our chatterbox it will usually accept this as a challenge. It may well be the case that it will choose to rear its head much more frequently. So long as we keep replacing the negative with a positive, we can train our subconscious into a new way of thinking. In time our chatterbox will start to take much more of a back seat and we will hear it much less frequently.

## The Belief System

As we can see, the human brain is an exceptionally complex tool. We carry certain beliefs through our life time that remain there, as they have never been challenged. In Horse Communication this can pose a problem for many different reasons. If we do not allow ourselves to communicate without judgment and not truly listening to what we are being told, we will never hear what is being said in its entirety. If we have already made a decision as to what is right or wrong for a horse, those beliefs can and will override what it is that we should be hearing. The reason for this again lies in our subconscious. When we hear something that doesn't agree with our own beliefs, we are taken out of our comfort zone which for many people takes them into un-chartered waters and quite literally out of their depth. Choosing not to hear it, and replacing it with a version of our own belief, is the obvious route it takes as a way yet again of trying to keep us mentally safe. When we choose to override our fear and let go of the egotistical part of us that tells us that we are always right, we leave ourselves open to hearing what the horse is truly saying.

For those of us that have horses, more often than not, we will have them for the honor of riding them. However, what if we can only afford one horse and they do not have the personality or desire that makes them want to be ridden? What if they have a bad back that we are unable to find the root cause of, or permanently 'fix'? If the horse is not showing refusal or pain when ridden, will we actually allow ourselves to hear that they do not wish to be ridden? As this would then go against our own wants and desires.

**The Ego in Perspective**

When we first start to communicate it can be a very life changing experience. For some of us it will be a very gradual process. For others it can be very quick and full blown in a matter of minutes or even seconds. It is very easy to become swept away in the excitement and to feel very good about our achievements. However, we need to remember at all times that what we are doing is very normal and natural and that each and every one of us has the ability to do this. We are all special in our own right and none of us, regardless of our ability, is better than another in the grand scheme of things. It is very easy to put ourselves high on a pedestal whilst looking down at others, something that we must avoid at all costs. If we choose to work with ego, the horses that we communicate with recognise it straight away. For some horses this can be very off putting. We need to remember the true reason why we want to communicate, which for most of us is a heart-felt desire. Staying true to ourselves is without a doubt one of the most important thing in any aspect of communication work.

*Without remaining true to ourselves, our integrity towards the horses becomes compromised.*

## The Authentic Self

In the navel area we have an energy centre often referred to as the Soul Self, Ancient Self or the 'Hara'. This part of us is our connection to our Authentic Self and our integrity, as well as our inner knowing and knowledge.

There are three areas of the body where we can experience our feelings. The head, the heart and the Hara. Each of these areas when they are focused on, will give us a good idea not only as to what we are feeling and 'how' we are feeling it, but also why and where our emotional focus lies.

**The Head**

This is the part of us that we use to rationalise these feelings and do what feels sensible, our logical thinking. It can cause us to fall prey to doing the logical thing, rather than the right thing for an individual and within our decision making.

**The Heart**

When connecting through the heart it can give us a romantic view and cause us to throw caution to the wind. Whilst we need to make sure that we are connected through our heart to make sure that our compassion is felt towards others, connecting through the heart alone can lead to poor decision making and selfishness when not done correctly.

**The Hara**

When we connect to our Authentic Self through our Hara, it gives us the knowledge to know what is right in the grand scheme of things. The next time you experience an emotional feeling take time to feel where about in our body you are experiencing it. You may feel a butterfly like sensation or a tingling or maybe just you will just have a knowing as to where the answer is coming from. Horses feel our energy and they sense our thoughts. They are instantly drawn to, and feel more comfortable with, the people who are not afraid to answer to themselves and choose to work with what they know to be true, rather than those who choose to cloud their own judgment by their false beliefs and negativity.

**The human brain is in very complex and consists of two hemispheres:**

**Left Hemisphere**

This acts as a tool for the conscious part of the mind. The left side of our brain deals with the day to day issues that we have and our logical thinking side such as reading, bill paying and thinking through problems. Others include: identity, grandeur, the sense of the terrific, defiance, display, perfection and speculation. Those that are logically minded will likely find this side of their brain to be the most dominant.

**Right Hemisphere**

This acts as a tool for the sub-conscious part of the mind. The right side of our brain deals with our creativeness, imagination, psychic ability and meditation. It is this part of the brain that is often used by some of the world's great artists, musicians and poets. It also deals with love for animals, children and home, self-love, dignity, sympathy, intuition, human nature and self-esteem.

The more creative minded of us will find that that is our dominant side of the brain. The more that we are able to use and integrate both of our hemispheres, the better mentally and emotionally balanced we will be.

## Brain Maps

Some of you may be familiar with brain maps. The brain is mapped in such a way that different areas are designed to deal with different ways of thinking, problem solving and movement, as well as how we feel and experience pain and the running of our physical body.

For everything that goes on within the body and our mind, there is an area in the brain that is mapped in order to deal with it and experience it.

Problems can arise when we fail to exercise and suitably use different maps of the brain. This can cause the brain map to shrivel and enables the neighbouring brain map to encroach upon its space.

The opposite is also true, meaning that when we have dominant parts to our brain, we may find that our dominant brain maps start to take over our less dominant areas. Thereby making the things that the less dominant areas deal with harder to work with.

By equally balancing the kind of work that we do and the way that we think, not only we will help to restore and balance our brain maps – we will also aid our own learning by helping our brain maps to work correctly, in turn making it easier to learn and experience. The is also true for the need for physical exercise and correct use of our body and movements.

If you are finding that you are having difficulty with gaining a connection or with your focus. Try regular mediation to help with this.

**Exercise**

Something as simple as visualizing a blank television scene will help. Try visualising a white blank screen with the television buttons along the bottom. Aim to maintain a clear white screen for as long as you can. Each time another vision or thought comes to mind, imagine pressing one of the televisions buttons that will bring you back to the white screen.

Try to gradually build up this process until you are able to maintain a clear white screen for several minutes at a time without interruption.

Once this has been achieved try 'tuning' to different stations using your buttons, decide before hand what it is that you wish to see (which channel) and allow your mind to take you to it, then returning to the clear white blank screen once the process has come to an end.

**Our imaginary television buttons can also have others uses such as:**

*Swapping channels*

*Turning up or down sound*

*'Tuning in'*

*Sharpness of image*

*Still or moving images*

# MEDITATION

Meditation is the action of quietening the mind. Something we do not have nearly enough of in our modern society. When we are in a meditative state we become much more relaxed. We switch over to the right side of our brain and our brainwaves begin to slow down. This allows us to become far more receptive to hearing, seeing and experiencing. Our brain is a muscle, when we choose not to use it fully it becomes lazy and less active. Meditation is often referred to as 'mind yoga' as it is a very gentle and gets the brain working again without any vigorous exercise or distraction.

The more we meditate, the easier it will become to find that quiet space in our mind. When we do this, our heart rate will slow down and our physical body will become far more relaxed. Whilst meditating, it is not unusual for people to keep being interrupted by unwanted thoughts. This will lessen in time.

Try working each day with the exercise from the previous chapter. The more you practice, the easier it will become for you. You may also like to adapt it, or think of other meditations that you can try.

# Training the Mind

During all of our waking and sleeping states there is an ongoing change of brainwaves states. These depend on what we are focused on and experiencing at the time. With practice it is possible to learn to train our brain to react and correspond to a desired state in order to control our own brain activity and therefore our focus and awareness. By learning to do this, with practice, it is possible to achieve heightened states of awareness and relaxation at will.

## Brainwave States

Beta is the highest mental state. It is associated with alertness and focused concentration or when engaged in mental activities, such as conversation or playing sports.

The Beta brainwave state corresponds to the frequency range of 13Hz to 40Hz.

The Alpha brainwave state is slower than Beta and is associated with reflection and relaxed mental focus, contemplation and visualisation.

It is also used for accessing deeper levels of creativity.

The Alpha brainwave state corresponds to the frequency range of 8Hz to 12Hz.

The Theta brainwave state is associated with meditation and relaxation. It is also used during light sleep and dreaming as well as creativity and stress relief. It has been shown that 30 minutes a day of residing in the Theta brainwave state dramatically improves our well-being and general health as well as enabling the need for less sleep.

The Theta brainwave state corresponds to the frequency range of 4Hz to 8Hz.

Delta is the lowest frequency state and is associated with dreamless sleep. It is possible to train yourself to remain awake in this state during deeper levels of meditation and awareness.

The Delta brainwave state corresponds to the frequency range of 0Hz to 4Hz.

The Gamma brainwave state is the most rapid of all the states. We briefly reach the Gamma state whilst receiving of high level information when processing occurs and during episodes of precognition.

The Gamma brainwave state corresponds to the frequency range of 40Hz or above.

## Binaural Beats

Binaural Beats were discovered by German born H W Dove. What he discovered was that when two signals of different frequencies are presented separately, that is one to each ear, it is possible that the brain will detect the phase variation between them. This then causes the brain to try and reconcile the difference that it finds, the difference being the Binaural Beats.

There are many CDs and Apps that offer binaural music for us to listen to. Some of these are in the form of classical music, whilst others may be in the form of the sound of rain with the binaural beats in the distance.

This kind of music is wonderful to have playing in the background whilst we are meditating, trying to sleep, or we are working on a project. It helps to relax us and aids in our ability to focus due to this.

**Example**

If a frequency of 100Hz is presented on one side and the frequency of 105Hz on the other, the brain will recognise the third frequency pulsing at 5Hz, which is the difference between the two frequencies.

A binaural beat will cause the brain to resonate with the frequency of the beat this is termed 'Frequency Flowing Response'.

By listening to a binaural beat it is possible to guide your brain to use a specific brainwave frequency by using the frequency following response method. If we are listening to a binaural beat pulsing at a frequency of 5Hz, which is a low Theta frequency, we can trigger our brain to resonate at that 5Hz frequency. This will automatically introduce brainwaves within the Theta range. The same is true for listening to a binaural beat pulsing at other frequencies corresponding to other brainwave states.

## Brain Synchronisation

When our left and right brain hemispheres start to resonate to a binaural beat in synchronisation we refer to it as 'whole brain synchronisation'.

This comes about when various parts of the brain begin to work together and resonate at the same frequencies, which causes neural pathways to fire more rapidly to enable information to flow more easily.

The energy patterns and electrical activity that form a pattern in the brain then become more wide spread, instead of remaining confined to certain areas.

## Dendritic Growth

Growth of our dendrites is encouraged by neural stimulation within the brain. Dendrites are the branch fibers that extend from the neuron / cell body. As these fibers increase so does the surface area that is available to receive information. The more dendrites our brain contains the more quickly and easily we can process information.

# HOW WE RECEIVE INFORMATION

Information about the horse's thoughts, feelings, experiences and health are all held within the horse's electromagnetic energy field. This is often referred to as the 'Aura'. Each individual piece of information is stored in the form of vibrational frequencies within this field.

By subconsciously reading these frequencies we are able to gain valuable information that is needed in order to help the horse. This is usually achieved whilst we are working in the Theta brainwave state. This information is then passed from our subconscious to out conscious in way that we can understand.

**There are three main ways in which this information is received:**

## Clairaudience

This is the ability to translate the information from the frequencies into words that we can understand. This may come in the form of single words or whole sentences. What we hear is our own interpretation of what the horse is saying. During this we will also be able to pick up on the type of personality the horse has by the way we are hearing them speak. Some horses may come across as quiet and say very little whilst others may be very talkative. Some people will hear the voice as if it were their own voice speaking whilst others will translate the information in more of an individual way better suited to the horse.

The voice may come across as very obviously male or female. As we are reading the horse's energy it can sometimes be confusing as to the horse's gender. It is possible for a male horse to come across as having a very feminine, gentle nature and vice versa. If the horse comes across as very annoyed, angry, or arrogant we can usually take this as a valuable sign that the horse has an emotional issue.

Some horses may be very talkative and be only too happy to share what they need to say. At other times you will find others less forth coming and need more of a question based approach in order that you may gain the information from them that is required.

## Clairsentience

This is the ability to 'feel' what the horse is both saying and feeling. This can be useful in a variety of different ways. Firstly, by working with clairsentience we are able to feel the horse's emotions and how they feel about certain things. For those people that have a strong sense of clairsentience the feelings that they pick up from the horse can be as informative as if they were actually hearing them speak. That is to say that rather than hearing actual words we feel a definite knowing or feeling of what the horse is saying and feeling.

Clairsentience is also extremely useful in assessing an horse's health, as this can allow us to feel within our own body any areas of physical discomfort that the horse may be experiencing. During our work with clairsentience when we are feeling the horse's emotions it is not unusual to become tearful and upset. At this point it is important to understand that these are the horse's feelings that we are experiencing - not our own, and that they will soon pass once the connection has come to an end.

## Clairvoyance

This is the ability to 'see' what the horse is showing us as well as being able to see the horse's energy and other such energy systems.

**This can be useful in a variety of different ways such as:**

*Being able to view blockages within the horse's energy systems.*

*Viewing land energies and other such systems that may well be causing the horse a problem.*

*Being able to view problems to do with the horse's equipment or tack.*

*Mentally viewing what looks like still photographs of the horse's past, or even what looks to be a mental video playing of an event in the horse's life.*

This can be a valuable tool to use when we are unable to hear or understand what the horse is saying, as we are then able to ask them to show us what they mean.

There is currently a school of thought that brings into question whether we actually see with our mind or with our physical eyes. Tests have shown that when the mind 'sees' or imagines we have the same chemical reactions within the brain, as we would do when seeing with our eyes. This gives us a firm understanding of why meditation can seem so real for us and how it can bring about such amazing results. This also brings into question whether we do truly see with our eyes or with our mind. Many of you will have heard people say that they have seen something with their 'third' or 'minds' eye. This is an energy situated in the centre of the forehead that allows us to see with the mind and internally within in us. When we are working with clairvoyance it is believed by many that this is where the energetic connection between what we are viewing and the actual viewing of it is made.

## Clairambience

This is the ability to be able to taste or smell what the horse is experiencing or describing. Whist working with clairambience you may be able to taste or smell the food the horse is eating, or the food they are explaining to you that they like or dislike. This will sometimes be accompanied by the feeling or sensation of the temperature of the food.

During your connection with the horse you may also experience other smells or tastes that they wish you to experience within their environment such as perfume, worn by the owner or hold-house chemicals that are bothering them. Clairambience can also be a valuable tool during body scanning. It may be that you mentally experience the smell or taste coming from a horse due to a medical problem such as an infection or stomach disorder.

# THE HORSE AND HUMAN LINK

Within all relationships we encounter in our lifetime there are valuable lessons to be learnt. We may find that we are faced with an argumentative parent or partner and within this kind of relationship, our lesson maybe one of mastering the art of understanding, acknowledging and eventually accepting the ways of others by complementing their own deficiencies - and they ours. In the same way we also have valuable lessons to learn from our horses.

**They can come into our lives for a variety of different reasons:**

*To teach us about ourselves as their problems may well resemble our own.*

*To mirror our behaviour by showing us how we are truly behaving and feeling.*

*To teach us how to love unconditionally, as horses pose no true threat to our feelings.*

*To enable us to feel at ease within a relationship when we have problems relating to other people.*

*To fulfill a karmic debt.*

Looking at it from this perspective our inter horse and human relationships are just as important as our relationships with people. Studying how someone treats a horse and whether this is done with compassion can give an insight into how that person relates to others. How they treat horses is a valuable clue to how they may treat other human beings. Studies have shown that children who abuse small animals are far more likely to grow up to commit violent crimes towards people than those who have a love for animals at a young age.

## What We Know To Be True

Anyone who has felt love for a horse and a special bond or connection when in their presence, will come to realise what an important role horses play in our lives. Not just the larger scheme of things, but also in each of our individual lives. In truth, when we come to understand what a horse truly is, rather than just what we perceive as their physical body, we come to a much deeper understanding of their true nature and the very point of their existence. Horses, like ourselves, are not just made of flesh and blood, but also of intricate energetic systems and many different levels of consciousness. There are some religions in the world that have denied the existence of the horse soul. If we choose to accept that the soul, or 'psyche' as it is often referred to, is part of the consciousness, or indeed its whole, then to deny the horse's soul existence would surely cause us to be in denial of the horse's ability to feel, express its self - or to even mentally exist. Looking at it from a logical point of view it is easy to see that this is not the case and that like ourselves, horses are more than just the physical bodies that many people still view them as.

Sadly this leaves the door wide open for many horses to be used as a 'tool' for those that wish to use and abuse them. By denying the existence of the horse's soul and therefore to a large degree their feelings, many will have little if any concern over how they choose to treat our horses. They will pull at their mouths, pull their heads into unnatural positions and beat them. How can they feel guilt or compassion when the horse does not feel it?

These kind of teachings only serve to condone and escalate that abuse that has no place in a civilised modern age and yet to this day, it is still taught and to a large degree accepted by many as the norm.

## How We Change

When this new realisation has come about it can open our eyes wide open to how we view the whole form of life and our interpretation of it. What is life? What is it all about? When we start to question the reason behind everything instead of taking as truth, what we read, or what we are told, then we have set ourselves truly on the path of exploring not only ourselves, but also everything that is alive and in existence. Once we are on this path we have the opportunity to learn and grow. We gain the ability to realise our own beliefs through our personal experience, rather than to follow anyone chosen leader or to adhere to the dogma of any one doctrine.

## Pure Clarity

We will never find a more clear or truthful understanding to fuel our beliefs than through our individual experience of a situation, be it of a physical or spiritual nature. These times of sudden realisation are often referred to as 'light bulb moments', as they can often quite literally feel like someone has switched a light on for you. When we receive such feelings of clarity we can take it as a valuable sign that we are indeed moving forward with our way of thinking, how we view the world and everything that exists in it.

## Going With Feel

As our intuition heightens and our sense of self-belief comes to the forefront - we learn to trust and believe in ourselves and what we have come to understand and know to be true. We may be told something or read something that may well not sit comfortably with us or resonate with us. We often term this as a 'gut feeling' when we experience it. We should listen to ourselves and take the appropriate steps as gut intuition can sometimes quite literally save our life!

In our modern education system we are taught to believe all that we are taught is truth. Sadly this is far from the case.

**For something to be truthful it needs to fulfill all of the elements of truth:**

*Logical and rational*

*Compassion for the individual*

*Practical*

*Allowing for the change between individuals – what is right for one may not be so for the next*

We also need to be open to the fact that is what is truth for us one day, may not be the same the next.

When we are in a constant change of growth and experience, what we know to be true will likely change as we learn to discover and unravel all of the possibilities.

## Selfless Love

Partly due to the ego and much of our believed self-importance it is common for selfishness to become an over inflated part of us. Within the ego everything we can be - from selfish to loving - has a part to play and every right to be there. Within every negative attribute we have a positive. When we form this balance between the two we help to level our way of thinking.

We will never be able to completely rid ourselves of our negative side – our shadow side. However, it is important to understand that an aspect of ourselves can only truly be negative when we choose to use it and display it in a negative way. When we use our negative aspects wisely they overstep into the positive areas of our life and have a positive effect on both ourselves and others.

In truth there is no such thing as a negative attribute – when it is used positively and wisely. It is only when we use such attributes for our own ends that it becomes negative and unproductive to anyone but our-self.

## Example

Our selfishness may be of service to us when people are applying unnecessary pressure to us through their own selfishness. Through our selfishness, or rather our 'need' for our own time, that may be viewed as selfishness. We find the courage to say 'no' and herein lies the positive attribute in the selfish attribute. Selfishness therefore may only be seen as selfishness within you by those that are selfish themselves. The same can be said for our other seemingly negative attributes also.

## Example

In the case of a human and horse relationship there will sadly come a time when it is right for the animal to leave the physical plane. For many of this it is a sad time. These feelings of sadness that our horse will be physically leaving us can be overwhelming. Many people try and hold on to their horses and keep them with them for longer, by allowing them to undergo invasive operations or to be given a course of drugs that are not in the horse's best interests. When there is no hope and the horse is truly suffering - be it mentally or physically - we then have the option of stepping in and saying 'enough is enough' and allow our animal to pass with dignity and love. Knowing that our decision was made through true love and understanding for our horse, rather than our own selfish desire to keep them with us. This gives much meaning to the phase 'sometimes love means letting go'.

# WHAT HORSES KNOW

Horses do not have such an active ego in the same way that humans do, nor do they carry out judgments in the same way as we do. They have a much more simplistic way of viewing things. By simplistic I am referring to their non-complicated way of viewing things and their ability to see things as they truly are, rather than any implication of lesser intelligence on their part. From an emotional point of view, they can sometimes have a problem with rationalisation as indeed we all can. But in general their thoughts about the on-going cycle of life are much closer to the truth than many of us would assume. Whilst their past experiences can play a very relevant part in their present, they live very much in the now. Instead they choose to live without critical judgment of others, preferring to see others for what and who they really are. They have a focus on what they know to be important, rather than wasting valuable energy on things that don't really matter. We can learn a lot from a horse's way of thinking when we choose to 'hear' them - rather than just 'listening' to what we expect to hear from them.

## How A Horse Receives Information

The way that a horse receives information is slightly different from our own. The information comes to them more in a 'feeling' type way. We still send the information in the same way as we receive it, using pictures, words and feelings, but it's more the feeling and intention behind the information we send that the horse is better able to understand. The clearer we are in both our thought and our intention, the clearer the information will be for the horse to understand.

## How Horses React To Request

Now that we can understand how the horse receives information during telepathic communication, we can see why it isn't always the case that a horse will carry out an act that is requested. Any request the horse receives from us comes by way of a feeling of the need to do something, or that something has changed that may need reacting to. The horse may not be aware that the request (or feeling) has come from yourself or another person. Once the horse has received the feeling, they then have to make a conscious decision on whether to act upon the feeling or to ignore it.

## Example

We can send a message to a horse that we wish it to walk forwards whilst giving it no physical cues. If the information is sent in clear enough detail to the horse so that it receives it, it will then get a feeling of needing to step forwards. If the horse can see no beneficial reason for moving forwards then chances are it will decide not to.

By not responding in the way you wish it to, the horse is not disobeying you. It simply has just not fully felt or understood the request, or it may be that they can see no logical reasoning behind fulfilling the feeling in a way that makes sense to them or they can see of being any benefit.

**Horse And Human Psychology**

Horse and human relationships, as well as playing a vital role in our growth, can also tell us a lot about ourselves. It is still commonplace for humans to see themselves higher up the evolutionary and intelligence ladder than horses. Some of the reasoning behind this is due to the horse not being able to (as we see it) communicate as clearly as we do. Within each species there is a clear understanding of what each other are saying from the noises they make to their body language, eye contact and sharing of thoughts. Just because we sometimes have trouble understanding what horses are saying, doesn't mean that they aren't communicating just as clearly as we are.

Horses have no need for such complex technologies as we use, no need for telephones or computers, as their way of long distance communication is far less complex and much more natural.

# 100th Monkey Syndrome

Japanese monkeys have been observed in the wild for 30 years on the island of Koshima. In 1952 scientists started to feed the monkeys with sweet potatoes that had been dropped in sand. Whilst the monkeys liked the taste of the raw sweet potatoes, they disliked the taste of the dirt and sand surrounding them.

Scientists observed that an 18 month old monkey, named Imo, found that she was able to solve this problem by washing the potatoes in a stream. She was observed doing this by other monkeys, thereby teaching her peers and family to wash their potatoes.

Over a period of time this was picked up by other monkeys and during 1952 through to 1958, scientists observed even young monkeys learning to wash their sweet potatoes. It was noted that older monkeys only learnt to do this through imitating and watching the younger monkeys who did this in their tribe. Consequently, it was found that some of the older monkeys still ate the dirty sweet potatoes.

In the Autumn of 1958 when a certain number of the monkeys were washing their potatoes (for arguments sake the number of monkeys being 99), then later that day the 100th monkey also learnt and started to wash them. By the late evening, practically all the monkeys in the tribe were washing them, as if the energy brought about by the realisation of the 100th monkey has caused some sort of ideological breakthrough.

The most surprising thing the scientists witnessed was that the monkey's habit of washing the sweet potatoes suddenly started to show itself overseas. It was observed that colonies of other monkeys on islands and a mainland troop from Takasakiyama then began to wash theirs too. Scientists then came up with the theory that when a number of animals or people come to a certain awareness, this may well be communicated at vast distances through telepathy (mind to mind).

The understanding being that if only a limited number of people understand something of importance and the '100th monkey' (we use 100th as the exact number is not known or may vary) does not recognise this, the information cannot be spread in this way so it then remains the conscious property and understanding of the original people or animals from which it originated from.

This example would then beg the question that if a large enough number of us were to come to a realisation of interspecies communication being a reality - over a period of time - the energy of that realisation would spread throughout the world and make it an active part of our lives. If this were to happen then it would have a huge impact on the way that many of us choose to view and respect all living things in existence on our planet. This would in turn challenge us to readdress many of our beliefs and how we treat one another, as well as all living species.

*What a nice thought!*

'Anthropomorphism' is a word that many of you will be familiar with. It basically means the assigning of human emotions to an animal. But do we actually assign human feelings to animals? Or rather are we just understanding that animals do have emotions in just the same way as we do?

We only have to look at the physical signals and behaviour of animals to see that they experience exactly the same emotions as we do.

## Examples

A mare that protests and becomes distressed when her foal is removed for weaning; she shows a maternal bond and sadness at that bond being broken.

A mare who grieves for her still born foal until such a time comes that she can come to an acceptance of its passing and covers it with straw as her final goodbye.

A horse that pines at the death of an owner shows it's upset and distress at the absence of that much-loved person.

A horse that is anxious after being abused shows fear and lack of trust and lives in the fear that it could happen again.

Horses appear to have not only all of the emotions we experience such as: grief, love, fear and resentment - but their way of thinking is without a doubt just as complicated and in-depth as our own. Not forgetting that horses also have all of the same Neuropeptides (emotional chemicals), not only in their brain, but also in their digestive tract - as humans do.

**Example**

Pearl is a 14 year old horse. She has been with her owner Julie for the past 8 years. She has never shown any signs of ongoing stress or behaviour problems. Not until the breakdown in relations between her owner and her owner's husband, at which time the husband left and no longer visited Pearl.

At this time Pearl became agitated and unsettled and would no longer be co-operative with her owner during handling or ridden work. This had been going on for around 18 months since the separation.

Pearl explains that she hates her owner because she made her 'dad' leave. (It is important to understand that as we are interpreting what Pearl is saying, that she views the husband as dad as he was the main male in her life who cared for her, and who she viewed as older. The same way that we may view an older male who cares for us as an 'uncle' even though they are not.)

Straight away, from how Pearl is speaking, we can see that she views her owner and her owner's husband as 'parents', as in those who care for her and her being in need of their nurturing. She sees herself as the child. So Pearl is angry with her 'mum' for making her 'dad' leave and breaking up the family unit and security.

Further talks with Pearl start to show up a picture of self-blame when viewed from another perspective. In similar human situations it is often a mislaid blame that is focused towards the mother. In situations such as this it is not uncommon that the child feels it is their fault that 'dad' didn't love or care for them enough so left them. Unable to cope with these emotions the only way that the child can cope with this, is to project the blame elsewhere, thereby taking the emphasis off of themselves.

This was indeed the case for Pearl. Deep down she felt that her 'dad' had left because he had not loved her enough to stay, or because of something she had done or thought she should have done. Once getting to the bottom of how Pearl is viewing the situation, it can be explained to her that she isn't to blame and help her understand what was truly behind it. Once this has been done the resentment towards her 'mum' subsides (As Pearl now sees her mum wasn't to blame but even more importantly that she wasn't either.) So Pearl's behaviour towards her 'mum' recedes and things go back to how they used to be once the realisation is gained.

Another way to view 'behaviour' from a horse, rather than seeing it as a behaviour problem, is to see it for what it is, a horse with a problem. Like children, horses develop behaviour problems as a way of showing something isn't right or comfortable for them.

### Example

A horse that bites strangers. It may well be that the horse has been abused by people in the past and when meeting strangers they feel vulnerable.

A horse that wind sucks (The action of opening the mouth and biting on a stable door or fence post whilst sucking in air.) maybe displaying signs of stomach discomfort / hunger or frustration.

A horse that is shut in a stable that obsessively bangs the door, weaves or box walks is showing stress at being kept in.

Within all of these examples we can see that the reason for such behaviour is due to an underlying problem and that the horse isn't using the behaviour to cause a problem. They are simply playing out their distress at the situation they find themselves in. Therefore, should these behaviours truly be classed as 'bad' behaviour?

Should we not instead be seeing them as valuable information from the horse that they are distressed and that changes need to be made in order to combat this, and enable them to feel emotional balanced?

When asking a horse about its behaviour problem, it is important to first view the question from the horse's perspective. Is the behaviour a problem to the horse? If the answer is 'no' then it is unlikely that the horse will understand what you mean by their 'behaviour problem'. In such cases it is often clearer to explain the behaviour that you are referring to and ask the horse why they feel the need to behave this way, rather than to label the behaviour as a problem, as this could lead to confusion.

It is also often the case that, like ourselves, horses can display upset through behaviour caused by a deeper subconscious memory or belief, that they are not consciously aware of. Sometimes this can lead to irrational fears and reasoning, or even phobias. Sometimes the cause of such things can be rooted in the horse's earlier years, or even in their past lives. The memories of which have stayed with them on a subconscious level.

Our own behaviour and outlook can have a huge impact on a horse's behaviour and their way of thinking. If we are of a negative mindset the moment that we connect with a horse, we will bog them down through our own negativity. The same can also be said for our other negative mental traits such as our anxiety and lack of consideration for another.

**When Horses Lie**

As horses think and feel in very much the same way as we do. They too can lie, both consciously and subconsciously, in a very similar way.

**Consciously**

This can happen when a horse is scared, ashamed or embarrassed to tell us something that they feel maybe used against them, or puts them in a vulnerable position. It may lead us away from an issue or line of enquiry that they do not wish to have pursued. By lying, they can lead us away from the truth thereby protecting themselves and possibly others. A horse choosing to lie may also be down to them wanting us to believe that a certain thing is true, in order that it brings an end to a dialog with us that that have no interest in participating in.

It is also not unusual for horses to tell us white lies such as they are feeling alright when we ask them how they are. Lies such as these may not be meant as a lie. It may just be the horse's natural way of answering due to them feeling that no one has cared about them in the past enough and that whilst you are asking them how they are, you are not actually interested in the truthful answer.

We can liken this to when another person asks us how we are. More often than not we will answer that we are 'fine' - even when we aren't.

## Subconsciously

This type of lying can be much harder to assess, as often even the horse isn't aware of it. It is usually used as a distraction to lead us (and often themselves) away from a very traumatic memory. Even if we suspect that the horse is lying and we choose to question them further on it, chances are they will still not be able to give us a truthful answer. Not because they don't want to; but because they literally 'can't'.

## Example

We may ask a horse if it is happy. It then assures us that it is. It may be that the horse in question is in fact unhappy, but doesn't want to acknowledge the fact, as if it does, it then has to deal with the reason for the unhappiness. The horse then consciously convinces itself that it is happy and that all is well as a way of self-guarding itself.

Most, if not all cases of subconscious lying, are a way of the horse protecting themselves. Their subconscious thinks that it is doing them a favor by hiding away details and feelings that may well bring about a negative emotion and upset. Unfortunately, when this happens, the negative vibration held within the energy field when allowed to stay for a long period of time, can start to distort the energy systems, eventually often leading to physical illness.

There are several ways that we can spot subconscious lying in horses. Sometimes it might be something as simple as a contradiction a horse makes during its communication that it later retracts or tries to 'tidy over' when asked about it. It maybe the case that you experience a 'gut feeling', or have a physical reaction, such a being covered in goose bumps or experience shivers down your spine. All of these should be taken as a sign that something isn't right within the conversation, although it should be noted that shivers down the spine and goose bumps can also be associated with confirmation of what is being said and that it is correct. These physical cues are created by the nervous system reacting to information. Over time, if you experience these feelings, you will learn to understand their meaning by assessing the information that is being received at the time they occur.

When you have learnt to recognise a subconscious lie, question the horse gently about it just as you would a person get them to look to the bigger picture about how they feel about the situation they have been talking about. Ask them to analyse it in a more open manner to see if they can understand the reason for it. If you are able to do this together, it might well be that you can get to the reasoning behind it and are able to deal with the issue at hand.

## The Reluctant Horse

Like people, some horses are more approachable than others and some are more open and willing to talk. How open to talking the horse is will very much depend on its personality. Some will be very talkative and chat away none stop hardly pausing for breath, whilst others will be less willing to comply and will work much better on an asking them questions basis.

Now and again you may come across a horse that isn't willing to talk which can be not only frustrating, but can also knock your confidence. Some horses can be very much like children in the way that they like to receive attention. A horse that's likes having people take notice of it and thrives on the attention it can bring itself may well not speak, as it is enjoying the coaxing it is receiving. In such cases, once the horse feels it has received enough attention, it will usually then choose to connect with you, or you may tell them you are disconnecting, and then they suddenly choose to engage with you.

Horses can also recognise our energy the moment we connect with them. If we are not in a very pleasant mood, or if we are feeling rushed or worried the horse may well pick up on this and feel that our energy is not a nice one to connect to. This can often be physically witnessed by the way that horses are drawn to certain people whilst they try and steer clear of or ignore others.

Some horses when they are not well practiced in communicating can sometimes find it hard to stay connected and focused. These can sometimes be the case in very young horses as well. In such cases it is often useful to communicate with an animal friend of theirs, who is often able to pass on the information on their behalf. Also, remaining patient is advisable. If they feel you are trying to hurry them it can bring them stress.

Another reason for a horse being reluctant to communicate with you is that by reading your energy when you connect to them, they are able to see that you are capable of seeing their true self. Like us, many horses choose to wear a mask falsely showing the world who they want to be seen as. This doesn't have to mean that they are bad in any way, just that they may have a lack of confidence in themselves that they do not wish you to see through.

When coming up against a reluctant horse that you have a problem communicating with, there are several different ways of trying to get them to engage in conversation with you. You can try asking them questions so if they are not very talkative, you can at least gain the information required in order to help them, or secondly, you can ask them what they would like to talk about, thereby leaving the door wide open and the ball in their court.

## Approaching the Horse

As we have already discussed, the moment we choose to connect to a horse they are aware of our energy. In order that we make ourselves as inviting as possible for the communication to take place, it is important that we are calm and focused. We need approach the situation by understanding how it feels to the horse.

*How do you feel when you meet a stranger and they start to talk to you?*

*Do you feel nervous, surprised or shocked?*

*Are you able to decide at that moment whether or not you feel comfortable in this person's presence and talking to them?*

This is exactly how it is for the horse. When we are happy and we are enjoying the situation the horse will pick up on the friendly energy that you are exhibiting. In most cases they will be comfortable enough to talk with you. If you are feeling under the weather, or are in a negative frame of mind, it is sometimes better to wait until it passes in order that your energy feels friendly.

# HOW TO INTERPRET

Information can come in many different forms including: Smells, pictures (both moving and still), or words and feelings. We all have our own unique way of communicating, and how we interpret the information we receive. When the information comes in a fragmented manner, it can quite literally feel like we are having to put together the pieces of a jigsaw puzzle. A horse may say that it 'feels' like its leg is broken. The emphasis here is then on the word 'feel'. Chances are the horse's leg is not broken. It is just that it uses this description as a way of helping us to understand the kind of pain or discomfort that is being experienced. When we see things such as colours - if we do not see as clearly as we do with our eyes, we can easily confuse them - such as dark brown and black, which can sometimes be confusing.

Sometimes a horse may say something that we don't understand. If this happens try asking the horse to repeat it. If the information is correct, even though not understood, or if it holds major importance, it maybe that it is accompanied by a physical sensation such as goose bumps or shivers - or even just an inner sense of knowing.

When communicating with horses it is not unusual

for them to bring up strange information. They may talk about a past life when they were another horse or even a human, and what happened to them at this time. Hear them out as this information is relevant to their healing. You will need to understand what happened to them, or what emotional or physical scars that life time left them with in order to aid them in moving forwards in the here and now.

From a medical point of view, we can choose mental tools with which to work that can aid us in our interpretation. When viewing a horse's joint we can choose to mentally view it as a strong beefy bone, or as a splintering chicken bone - depending on how that join is physically, in order to access what state of repair it is in. With areas of soreness or inflammation it is possible to use a 'colour chart' ranging from healthy tissue colour, through to red and then purple and brown. This can give us a clear insight into the state of the area. For example: red may be an area of inflammation or infection, or a deep purple or brown may show us dead flesh or dried blood in that area, whilst grey may represent toxins.

The key to communicating is to take on board everything that the horse says and to analyse it in depth afterwards. If you can't make out the meaning of something at the time, anything we don't understand we can easily question the horse about in more depth later on. When we have limitations in our understanding and our ability to interpret, it can come about through a lack of terms of reference from our subconscious memory banks - especially from a medical point of view. The more knowledge we have about anatomy, holistic medicine, therapies, allopathic medicine and the spiritual world - the more easily we will be able to interpret the information in a clear manner, so that it makes more sense to us.

## When Something Doesn't Feel Right

Sometimes during a communication something won't feel quite right. It's not always what the horse says or how it says it. Sometimes it might just be a gut feeling that we have. When experiencing what you recognise to be your gut feeling - take it on board. Gut feeling is a very strong intuitional tool to have and when used it can prove very useful. Question around the situation and play detective to see if you can get to the bottom of things. Often when something doesn't feel right - it isn't!

## Horse Emotions At Cellular Level

Cellular level vibration and emotions all carry a vibrational signature. It could be that a horse was tethered and grazing at a roadside when it was hit by a car. As each cell of the body has its own unique intelligence separate from the brain, the cells of the body during this time will access the body to see what isn't normal for it at the time of trauma. It may well be that the cells recognise the food being eaten at the time as a foreign body. When this happens it may well be that the cells choose to recognise such foods as an allergen. If this is the case, it may be that in the future when the same food is eaten, the animal will have the physical symptoms of a food allergy or intolerance. In the same way, if a horse has an accident that is emotionally traumatic for it, the emotional cellular memory of the incident can stop the injury from healing quickly, due to the energy of the cells being stuck in trauma shock.

As well as accidental trauma manifesting problems, so can pure emotional trauma. When a horse holds negative emotions within their energy field, the vibrational frequencies over time will distort the homeostasis of the physical body. This will usually lead to physical illness over time. For most, if not all illnesses, there may be both physical and emotional symptoms. By addressing the emotional discord through healing, we can help to heal the physical body too, by going straight to the route of the problem

## Other Examples

Horses that mentally maintain their lameness as a way of avoiding being walked or ridden. It may sound odd - but it is not as uncommon as you would expect.

Horses who don't want to get well, as illness either serves them a purpose (attention), or they feel that they don't deserve to be well.

Mares that don't fall pregnant because they are scared - maybe due to them experiencing a bad time during their own birth, or a trauma whilst giving birth previously.

## Non-Violent Communication and Training Methods

There are no end of training methods available to use, but are all such methods in the horses' best interests? In recent years there has been a resurrection in Natural Horsemanship training methods. On first inspection of many such named methods, the horse appears to understand what is being asked and physical results are seen. But what is the horse experiencing and thinking?

With many of the training methods the horse is put in a situation where it has a limited choice in how it can react. In some cases when the desired outcome is not seen, gadgets are applied that cause tension or pressure to the horse, either mentally or physically. If the horse has no intention of allowing physical discomfort to come into play, they are given little choice as to whether or not to comply. With these kinds of training methods there is always an implied 'If you don't do what I ask, I will do this to you'.

Regardless of whether or not the implied threat is carried through or not - it is still a threat. This could well be considered violent communication. There are many gadgets to help 'control' behaviour on the market.

These include: Nut cracker throat collars used to stop a horse wind sucking (gulping air), head collars that cause tension over the nose when pressure is applied to the lead rope, or even head collars with metal studs around the headpiece that runs across the top of the head and over the sensitive poll.

Many of these gadgets will bring about the desired affect - but is it for the right reason?

By using such barbaric tools we are simply masking the issue instead of assessing, identifying and dealing with the underlying issue. The use of such tools shows a lack of logic and obvious ignorance, as well as a lack of compassion from the person using such a tool.

Through communication we can ask the horse why they feel the need to behave in such a way. This then enables us to address the problem in a kind and sympathetic manner. There are so many routes to solving problems, all we have to do is identify them, find the cause, and then the issue can be handled kindly.

When training horses or seeking a new training method, try to view the psychology of it through the horse's eyes.

*How would it make them feel?*

*Does it give them time to think?*

*Why is it working?*

*Would you consider it violent (A threat being implied or carried out) or is it non- violent - where the horse will see a reward for good behaviour and be able to make safe choices?*

When horses are put in a situation where they can think things through and see a reason why the new improved behaviour would be of benefit to them, you are much more likely to have a willing training partner. The main thing is never lose sight of why they display such behaviour in the first place. What we perceive as a behaviour problem, may not be viewed as such by the horse. Looking at their environmental situation and our own behaviour can easily rectify many everyday behaviour problems shown by our horses.

All too often the simplest of changes in daily routine, home environment and the care-giver can bring about massive changes.

# CONDUCTING A SESSION

Firstly, before we begin to communicate we must prepare ourselves both mentally and physically. We must decide whether or not we intend to communicate in person with the horse physically present, or through distance communication. Both will bring about the same results, but other things also need to be taken into consideration.

If you are communicating with a horse that is likely to constantly nudge you, you may find yourself distracted, or if you are in a field or stable in the middle of the winter and are cold, you might find that again you have problems concentrating. Other things such as time spent travelling also need to be weighed up.

Whether you choose to be in the physical presence of the horse in question or not, the process is still the same. There are several ways we can choose to conduct the session. It maybe that you decide to let the horse run the session and do all the talking. The problem you may find if you intend to work this way is that the horse might not be particularly communicative, or that the information the owner is looking for may not be forthcoming. By asking the horse what they wish to say we can leave the door open for anything we might otherwise miss hearing.

This works rather well when followed by a question and answer type session where we ask the horse things the owner wishes to know about, so that we can pass on the answers to them.

## In Person

Sit or stand with the horse that you wish to communicate with. You may find that you wish to touch them in order to connect with their energy more easily, or it may be that you find it easier to imagine them in your minds eye

Close your eyes and take a few deep breathes.

Allow your energy to flow outwards towards the horse, with the intention that they will feel it and choose to connect with you.

Then relax as the information comes to you in the form of words, pictures and feelings.

When you feel the need to ask a question, phrase it in a positive way so that if it is received in a fragmented manner, no vibration of any negative words such as 'hurt' or 'danger' will be experienced by them.

Think of it being like a parcel that you are sending someone with lots of different components. In order that they are able to fit them together correctly, all of the components need to be present. This means that when we send a question to a horse or make another form of request, we need to make sure that all of the information is there.

For example: If we are asking them about food, as well as asking them the actual question, we may send them the image of their food bowl along with an additional question such as, 'how do you feel about it'.

Once the communication has come to an end, remember to 'thank' the horse for communicating with you.

**Distance Communication**

Sit or lie comfortably in a warm room without any distractions such as telephones or radios.

Close your eyes and picture the horse's face looking at you as if they need to tell you something.

Send out the energy and intent that you are open and willing to hear them.

Alternatively you might find it easier to close your eyes and picture yourself stood in a field or a stable, as you watch them mentally enter it and stand beside you. Again, remember to phrase the information you are sending them in a positive way and 'thank' them again once the session has come to a close.

## All Thought Is Energy

Now that we are ready to start to communicate with our horses, we need to understand the energetic dynamics behind it.

Every thought we have, every word we speak and every single intention that we have - carries a vibrational signature. When intention is put behind a word it can have a positive or negative effect. This will depend on the type of word it is and the expression behind it. The words we send out and receive when communicating aren't so much what the horse receives from us. It is more the energetic dynamic behind the spoken word and what it means. We can understand this by accessing how we feel when people speak to us. Not only by the words they use but also by how those words make us feel when used with intent and emotion.

## Example

If someone tells us that they hate us, it will cause us a very different feeling to when someone tells us that they love us.

So when we are communicating in order to help the horse to feel as comfortable as possible, we need to phrase our thoughts and words in a positive way.

'Nothing will hurt you in your stable. No one will ever hit you again when you are in there'.

The above statement when received in a fragmented manner by the horse can bring about negativity due to these parts: 'Hurt you' and 'hit you'.

We can adjust the statement to: 'You will always be safe in your stable and will always feel comfortable with people in there'.

This will give the statement an overall positive feeling.

Negativity, or the type of negativity can have a bigger impact on some horses than others. For some horses emotional discord is far more distressing than physical disharmony and vice versa. What one horse might call a 'smack', another horse might see as a 'beating'. In the same way, two horses who have had their owner throw a food bowl at them in temper, may view it in a different way due to the intent behind it. One may view it as distressing and see the frustration behind it and feel scared. Whilst another may feel their human's emotions and know that they aren't angry at them. They are frustrated and upset about something else so that the horse knows that this display is not aimed at them personally. The outcome due to feeling the emotion and intent of throwing of the food bowl at them, can therefore bring about a different feeling about the situation, and so a totally different outcome as to how they feel and view it emotionally.

The moment we choose or intend to connect with a horse, they know how we are feeling at that time. This will have an influence on our energy and the way in which the horse interprets it. If we are feeling under the weather, negative, angry or in any other way not positive, we are not feeling as comfortable to connect with as we could do, and the horse may not be so willing to communicate with us. By assessing our own feelings and dispelling with any negative thoughts we are holding onto, we make ourselves far more approachable and comfortable to connect with. At this time we also need to assess our intention and our integrity.

*What is our intention?*

*Is it because if we can find out about the horse's physical illness, we might be able to spare ourselves from an expensive veterinary diagnosis?*

*That we want to impress people?*

*Or is it that we genuinely have a heartfelt desire to help?*

Whatever your intention behind your communication, the horses will know the moment that you connect with them. If your intentions aren't of the highest integrity, the communication my lack in information the horse may otherwise have passed on.

When we choose to communicate for the wrong reasons, it may well be that whilst the horse is happy to talk with us about day to day issues and about medical problems. It may not feel comfortable enough to discuss deep emotional issues even though these may well be the underlying problem behind all of its other problems in the first place

**Taking a Case Study**

Before we start our case study, we must first decide which way we would like to work. This can either be with a question and answer type approach, or we may decide that we just want to see what the horse has to say for themselves.

It might also be a good idea to discuss which type of approach the horse's person feels would be more beneficial.

At the beginning of a communication, it is always a good idea to ask the horse's owner if they would like you to briefly explain horse communication and how it works so that they can gain a better understanding of what is likely to happen.

Any previous information that the owner offers is useful, but not always necessary. Although, if information is offered, it may help us fit pieces of the jigsaw puzzle together and also to help us assess how best to phrase our questions.

However, the information that is passed on by an owner in some cases may just be their view of the presenting problem. Due to this it is important to be open to the fact that the owner's information at times may be incorrect and the horse may view the issue in a totally different light.

Remain open to any information that the owner gives you, but by the same token do not allow yourself to be swayed by it and I what you hear from their horse.

# Recording

It is always useful to keep a written record of any communications that you do to enable you to refer back to at a later date. This might be so that over time you can assess how the horse is progressing, or simply so that you don't forget any important pieces of information that you receive. By making a carbon copy of the communication or a photocopy, we then have both a copy for our self and also one for the owner. Emailing as a Word Document is also a good idea as we can then pass one copy on and file another for our records.

Making notes whilst communicating can be very difficult and distracting. If you have someone with you whilst you are communicating, ask them if they will do the writing for you so that you can give the communication your undivided attention.

It is always advisable where possible that you fill out as much of the communication sheet as you can at the beginning, so that you have all of the information needed at the start of the communication. The actual communication information and any additional information can then be added during or after the communication has taken place.

Another way that you may wish to work is through automatic typing or writing. With practice, some of you may find that you are able to type as you communicate as a way of linking the two skills together. As the answers come to you, you simply type them or write them, until such a time as the communication comes to an end.

Automatic typing is not so much only about typing what you hear, but also an innate knowing of what to type, hence the term 'automatic' as you literally just type without giving it much thought at the time due to it being so automatic.

**Example**

Owners Name

Address

Telephone Number

Email Address

Date of Communication

Animals Name

Species

Breed

Colour

Age

Any known problems

Any known illnesses

Any previous information given by owner

**Example Questions**

How does he feel emotionally?

How does he feel physically?

Is he in any pain?

Does he feel his food is right for him?

How does he feel about our relationship?

Does he enjoy his training?

Is there anything he needs to tell me?

Does he know it is safe to voice his concerns?

Does he feel he has recovered alright after his operation?

Some people also find that the owner is a useful link for them in order that they can tune in to the horse more successfully. You may also choose to use what we refer to as a 'witness'. This is something that has a connection to the horse such as a photograph of the them, or a piece of the horse's hair. Some people feel that the witness helps them to establish a better or easier first connection to the horse.

Audio recording is more often used as the communicator's record of the communication. Sometimes you might find this your preferred way of working and you make a copy of the recording for the horse's owner. The problem with verbally recording a communication is that there may be long gaps within it when your focus is on the communication with the horse. You may become distracted by sorting out the words and phrases you need in order to get the information across.

If you do decide to use the verbal form of recording for your communication, you first need to decide what format it will take.

Do you intend to record or write down contact details and other relevant information before hand or record it at the time?

Are you just communicating with the horse and repeating its words in the same format as they come to you?

Or are you going to first record the question and

then communicate with the horse, followed by recording the answer?

An alternative and easier approach to this is to still have a written record of all the answers that are to be asked, then just record all the answers as they come. If this is your preferred way of working, then any CD should be marked with the horse's and owner's name. The date of the communication and be kept with a written record of the questions that have been asked.

**When Horses Don't Want To Well**

It is a sad fact that many horses remain in ill health, be that of a physical or emotional nature and through their own making. It maybe that the horse in question has a low self-esteem and for whatever reason feels that they do not deserve the special attention and treatment required. The low self-esteem may have come from many years of neglect and not experiencing a loving owner, or from years of being told or made to feel that they are useless and unworthy. When we come across a situation like this it is our job to explain to them just how much they are loved, how much they are cared for, and pass on information to the owner about how they can aid them further. This may well be in the form of Hands on Healing, or some form of other therapy such as Zoopharmacognosy, but reassurance goes a long, long way.

## Munchausen By Proxy

This is a psychological illness whereby people use their horse's distress or illness to gain attention for themselves. It may also show in the form of putting their horse on 'display'.

The physical form of the illness is easier to identify as it often presents obvious physical symptoms. This can range between something such as someone dying their horse's mane pink - to physically causing harm to their horse by wounding them, or feeding them food or medicines that they know to be harmful.

The energetic form of the illness usually involves a subconscious desire on the side of the owner to maintain their horse's illness. This is done on an energetic level by constant draining them of their energy in a bid to keep them weak. In this case it is unlikely that the owner will be aware of what they are doing.

## So What Is Munchausen By Proxy?

Munchausen by Proxy is a psychological illness whereby the sufferer uses their animal (or child) to gain attention for themselves. Usually the person in question will have something missing from their life that is unfulfilled. Often this is through not receiving attention from other people. By physically or energetically (subconsciously) maintaining their horse's illness, they gain people's pity and understanding that then aids them in feeling better about themselves. Many people who have this disorder on a physical level are aware that they are doing it, though they may not always be sure of the reasoning behind it or have control over it. People who do it on an energetic (subconscious) level are usually, though not always, unaware. Similarly, people can drain a horse of their energy as a way of boosting their own, rather than choosing to channel it from elsewhere.

## Symptoms

The owner (or another person) administering the horse with knowingly harmful foods or medications - usually on a regular basis.

The owner who chooses not to get medical attention the horse needs.

A person who pushes their horse out in front of them, using them to hide behind. By people noticing the horse - the owner will then be noticed also.

An owner who continuously talks about their horse to the point that they lose friends as there is no other topic of conversation.

People who take their horse from Vet to Vet, from

Therapist to Therapist, then claim that no one has been able to help them, but they know that you are 'the one' who can. Usually this will involve the changing of many vets and therapists over short period of time so that the relevant people aren't able to have long enough to treat the horse with any chance of success.

The owner who says that money is no issue and then spins a very long tale about how much they love their horse and how much money they have spent on them with no improvement seen. This may even be over a span of years.

The owner who telephones you any time of night or day, trying to gain as much sympathy from you as they can, with their woeful stories of how things aren't improving with their horse.

Obviously, some of these symptoms can be totally genuine with no cases of Munchausen behind them, but more often than not, when three or more of these symptoms are seen, there will be an element of the problem existing.

When someone is harming their horse in such a way it can be very distressing for us as an outsider looking in. We can feel helpless to do anything. In the case of physical harm being caused we can notify the relevant authorities, but with the energetic form of this mental illness there is a lot less that we can do to help. That is unless the horse's owner chooses to recognize and acknowledge the fact that they have an illness. In order to stop the horse's owner from draining us in the same way, we need to step back a little and approach the whole situation in a professional manner, so that we don't find ourselves caught up in the owner's self-made drama. It can be very hard to help a horse in these circumstances, as on an energetic level much that we do to help will be counteracted by the owner. One thing that we can do is wrap the horse up in golden healing light to help keep them safe. Then explain to them that we understand about their situation, that we are always open and willing to listen whenever they need us.

# BODY SCANNING

Body Scanning can be used for many different things. It can be used for looking for blockages and the state of the physical body, location of discomfort and stiffness, as well as looking at the make-up and disruptions of the horse's energy systems.

The Etheric Body is energetic in its make-up and consists purely of energy. It is made up of several different energy systems.

The Aura exists around the physical body. It has many different layers, the main ones being:

**First Layer – The Physical Plane**

This relates to the base or root chakra. It bridges the connection between the energy body and the physical body.

**Second Layer – Emotional Body**

This relates to the sacral chakra. It is associated with the vibrations of inner feelings.

**Third Layer – Mental Body**

This relates to the solar plexus chakra. It is

associated with the vibrations of the ego, mental thought processes and the horses' thoughts.

## Fourth Layer – Astral Body

This relates to the heart chakra. It is associated with the horses' expressions of feeling on a mental, emotional and physical level.

## Fifth Layer – Spiritual Plane

This is related to the throat chakra. It is the horses' blueprint for their lower etheric body.

## Sixth Layer – Celestial Body

This relates to the brow chakra. It is associated with the horses' 'enlightenment'.

## Seventh Layer – (Ketheric) Casual Body

This relates to the crown chakra. It is associated with the horses' connection to the divine.

## Eight Layer – Cosmic Plane

This is associated with to the horses' past and future karma and is their link to the Akashic records.

## Ninth Layer – Soul Body

This is associated with the connection between where the horse is now and what they perceive as heaven.

## Tenth Level – Integrative Body

This is associated with the connection between the physical and spiritual worlds. It is able to disconnect from the physical body to enter into the astral realms.

It is not unusual to find as many as 14 auric layers within the horse's aura - sometimes even more.

## Chakras

These are energy vortices in the energy body of the

horse. Horses have both primary and secondary chakras. When the chakras are out of balance through physical or emotional ailments healing can help to restore the balance and repair.

- ① Base - B
- ② Sacral - S
- ③ Solar Plexus - SP
- ④ Heart - H
- ⑤ Throat - T
- ⑥ Third Eye - TE
- ⑦ Crown - C
- ⑧ Brachial - B
- ⑨ Second Heart - SH
- ⑩ Thymus - TH
- ⑪ Soul Star - SS
- ⑫ Stellar Gateway - SG
- ⑬ Home Star - HS
- ⑭ Earth Star - ES
- ⑮⑯ Balance Left/Right - BL/R

# Meridians

These are energy pathways throughout the body some of which are linked to major organs. They are used in Chinese Medicine for Acupuncture and Acupressure treatments. There are 66 meridians in all. Only 14 of these meridians are commonly known of and used. Different meridians in the body carry slightly different energy. We will focus on the most commonly used meridians that are known to carry 'Chi' throughout the body. Each meridian has a partner meridian that it works in conjunction with and that it has connections to.

**Jing** Creative and Generative Energy

**Chi** Life Force Energy

**Shen** Spiritual Energy

**Each type of these energies are made up of five elements:**

**Water Element Meridians**

Bladder and kidney
Colour: Blue

**Wood Element Meridians**

Liver and gall bladder

Colour: Green

**Fire Element Meridians**

Heart and small intestine
Colour: Red

**Earth Element Meridians**

Stomach and spleen
Colour: Orange

**Metal Element Meridians**

Lung and Large intestine
Colour: Grey

**The Conception Vessel and the Governing Vessel**

Colour: Black or white

The Etheric Body is the blue print for the physical. When parts of the energy system become blocked or disrupted, over time, the imbalances can filter through to the physical body, often leading to ill health. By maintaining them in a healthy balance we can aid physical, mental and emotional well-being.

There are several ways that we can scan a horse. We can choose to scan them physically or mentally, in person, at distance, or choose to scan the physical body or the energy systems.

## Body Scanning In Person

When we are in the company of the horse that we are going to body scan we have several options: We can choose to hold our hands on or just above the horse, to see what physical sensations we pick up.

## These may include:

*Tingling*

*A knowing of where to place our hands and for how long*

*Electric shock type feelings*

*Heat or cold*

It may even be that we can see energetic disruptions over certain parts of the body that may indicate an issue.

*Just go with your intuition as to what needs to be done.*

We can also choose to mentally scan the horse. Often closing our eyes helps us to focus, as when we have our eyes open we can revert back to the wide awake Beta brainwave state. Alternatively we can move our eyesight around the horse's physical body, taking note of any areas that we are drawn to. If you find this difficult try relaxing a little more and don't try too hard.

## Distance Body Scanning

This can be done using the same method as I have described above. Try closing your eyes and visualizing the body of the horse. You do not have to do this in fine detail and it is often the case that viualising just the silhouette of their body is enough.

Now look for any areas that stand out for you.

As an example: you may see areas of white fog indicating muscular issues, or areas of red fog indicting deep rooted pain.

It is always useful to have some ready prepared diagrams of the outline of a horse showing different angles that you can draw your finding onto and use as a recorder for later reference and to see what changes occur over time.

## Scanning Tack and Other Equipment

The same method that we use for scanning the body and energy systems may also be used for scanning objects such as saddles, bits and rugs.

As well as mentally associating the object with the

horse and feeling which part if any maybe suspect, we can also mentally put the piece of equipment on the horse (such as saddle or a bit) to check the fit of it. If the horse is showing any signs of discomfort around the areas that the equipment fits, try scanning the physical body and then the equipment to see if the areas showing up correspond. For example: a sore area on a horse's back and their saddle.

Then try taking the saddle out of the equation mentally, and see if this same area still shows up on the physical body. If it does not, it way well mean that the soreness is already existing and that the saddle itself, is not to blame for the soreness.

A tip! If a horse tells you they do not need the dentist do not take their word for it – instead have a look yourself to see if there are any issues. A horse that doesn't like having dental examinations based on past experience. May feel it is better to suffer instead, which is not always the best outcome for them.

## Symbolic Signs and Meanings

Due to how our mind chooses to interpret and also due to our own level of understanding, it may be that sometimes things might not come through as clearly as we would like. For instance, if we have a poor level of knowledge about the physical body it maybe that we choose to interpret it in a symbolic manner.

## Example

If we are viewing the horse's liver and find it to be unhealthy, we may see it as shriveled or in a different colour - such as green or grey. This could be an indication of toxins or disease.

In time the symbols that are personal to you will be repeated when you come across the same problem over and over. It is very often a case of putting pieces of the jigsaw together to decipher what they mean. The more you practice and the better knowledge you have of the physical body, energy systems and other therapies - the easier and clearer the information will be presented to you. If at any time you come across something that you don't understand, keep a mental note of it as well as writing it in the horse's records. Chances are, once you come across it for a second time, or have had more time to think, the meaning behind it will become apparent.

# EARTH ENERGIES

Horses are very sensitive to energy and fluctuation in energy. Often when they can feel energies it can appear alien to them, as they are not always able to sense what they are related to or their source. In some cases they are unable to understand whether they are positive or negative for them. In many cases this can bring about a feeling of uncertainty or even panic and avoidance. Especially in the case of accident black spots and the energies emitted from old slaughter barns.

The earth consists of many types of land energies. Many can be likened to charkas or meridians that exist in human and animal bodies. However, many other land energies exist, such as those given off by standing stones and old religious sites.

This can sometimes cause horses react in strange ways. Animals such as dogs and horses are most widely affected due to covering more ground. Cats of course often cover large distance and may be affected. It is just that we aren't often there to witness their change in behaviour ourselves. Also, as they are free roaming, cats are able to avoid these areas much more easily.

# Symptoms of Land Energy Behaviour

*Spinning in circles*

*Rearing*

*Reluctance to pass certain areas on a singular or repeated basis.*

*Refusing to enter certain fields or buildings, or certain areas of them.*

Horses that experience earth energies often describe them as causing sensations such as tingling, trickling, electric shocks or just as a strange atmosphere. Some horses are able to see earth energies and may choose to describe them to you in the form of colours and pictures. This can help you to understand the type of energies that you are seeing.

When coming across a horse that appears nervous or is suffering from behaviour problems due to earth energies, it is advisable to help the owner to find someone who has knowledge of how to work with these energies. This maybe someone qualified in Geomancy or maybe a Crystal Therapist who can choose crystals to stop the horse feeling the sensations, or who can crystal grid the areas involved.

The land energies will either be mapped through the

Therapist being able to see the actual energies, or through them dowsing them.

One of the most interesting cases that I have worked with, is a case of a horse that was referred to me by another animal communicator due to his spinning in the road in complete panic. He had become dangerous to both himself and his rider.

When I communicated with him he told me (stressfully) that if the sparks hit his legs - then he might die. Obviously his physical well-being was not in any danger from these energies other than through a potential accident due to his physical responses. But the level of fear that it was creating for him was profound. Due to this his owner was no longer taking him out to be ridden due to his unpredictable behavior.

I was able to do a Shamanic journey to find out what was needed to solve this issue for him. I was shown that he needed a piece of rose quartz crystal as well as a piece of amethyst attached to his bridle and saddle. That this would set up and create an energy field that would soften these sensations for him.

It worked – he was able to be ridden out again without any issues and the last I heard several years later, he was still ridden out with his crystals in place.

## Spiritual Problems

Horses can suffer from spiritual problems in much the same way as humans do. These can come in two different forms.

## Disconnection from the Transpersonal Self

In such cases the horse may feel 'lost' and disconnected from itself. By not being fully mentally and spiritually integrated, horses can be open to psychological disorders such as Multiple Personality Syndrome and depression.

If you work with healing, aiding the horse in grounding through his Earth Star chakra and connecting through his Crown, Soul Star and Stellar Gateway may help.

## Outside Spiritual Influences

This can very much fall into the realm of spirits. Horses may be seen to be acting in strange ways, such as running dangerously from apparently nothing in blind panic or lunging viciously at something that can't be seen. Although lesser symptoms may be seen, such as: snorting at what appears to be mid-air to avoiding certain places. Horses that encounter such problems might tell of 'something' chasing them. Something they can see, or changes in temperature for not obvious reason whilst they are stationary in one place.

In such cases it is advisable to contact someone who works in the field of removing these types of energies. Some of these energies are only a problem when they are upsetting the horse. These could be energies such as another horse that has died but wants to stay close to them, or who had lived there previously and still sees the place as 'home'. Whilst not threatening in nature, if the horse is unable to understand what it is feeling, it may become a problem for him and create fear and discomfort.

# WORKING WITH OTHER THERAPISTS

As much as it is interesting and rewarding working with many kinds of therapies, if we choose to cover too many fields, we can spread ourselves too thinly. As you develop in your work you are likely to meet other Therapists and Healers that you feel drawn to. This can be very useful - not only from the point of view that you are able to pass work and clients to each other, but also that you can share your ideas and experiences.

Each one of us has our own unique way of working that will have a place to fill in the bigger picture. We all give off slightly different energies and have different ways of working and what suits one horse may not suit another.

# Therapies

Here is a list of commonly used therapies that you may well find useful to aid the horses that come into your care. All of these therapies can be worked with in a 'text book' or intuitive way, the latter often being the most beneficial to the horse.

Many, but not all Therapists, will have an element of energy work and intuition within their therapy depending on their own level of understanding and advancement.

## Chiropractic

This therapy involves the manipulation of the body to help realign the spinal column. Sometimes this can take several treatments as in order for the bones to stay in place, the muscles must be strong enough to hold them there. If a horse has been misaligned for a long period of time, the muscles would have adapted to holding the body in this new way. It can take twenty-one days for the muscles to reform and be able to hold the body into its new and correct alignment.

## Homoeopathy

The idea behind homeopathy is that when using it, we are treating 'like with like'. The dis-ease or illness held within the body will hold a certain vibrational signature unique to that illness. The idea being that by treating the body and energy systems with the 'same' vibration - the vibration is then cancelled out.

Like all therapies and medications that are energetic in nature, Homoeopathy should only be used by those who are very experienced and educated in its uses. Currently it is only legal for a suitably qualified Veterinary Surgeon or the horse's owner to prescribe such remedies for a horse.

## Herbalist

It is believed by some people that for each illness or dis-ease, there is a natural plant source to help combat or solve the problem. Each herb used has a medicinal property that when used correctly and in the right dosage, can help the body to correct itself, release toxins, or provide itself with the nutrition needed. Herbs have been used for many thousands of years in Chinese Medicine with often amazing results.

Horses have an inbuilt intuition as to the healing ability of herbs. When left in a natural environment they will often be seen self-medicating. When we make herbs unavailable to horses within their everyday environment, we then of course take away the availability for them to self-medicate. In the case of grazing horses, pastures are best left naturally without the use of weed killers. Much of what we consider to be weeds – is in fact medication for our horses.

## Example

Chamomile - Calming and soothing

Milk thistle - A good liver tonic

Dandelion - Helps support the urinary system

Plantain - High in nutrition similarly to linseed

## Safety Note:

Ragwort is often found in grazing. It is so toxic that it is listed on the dangerous weeds act and carries heavy fines if it is left to go to seed and allowed to spread. It is easily recognizable due to its bright yellow flowers.

When dried and baled in hay, it can break down into small pieces so that the horse has no choice but to eat it, it then also tastes less bitter to the horse. Ragwort has accumulative toxins, so sadly the liver damaged caused may not been seen until such a time that it reaches 75%.

Sycamore and Yew trees should also be removed from the horse's environment. Please keep in mind that Sycamore seeds can be blown long distances and can be highly toxic.

## Spiritual Healing

This therapy involves the Healer channeling Chi (Life Force Energy) towards and into the horse. This may be carried out by touching the horse or by holding the hands slightly away from them. Energy is then channeled from the Universal Energy Source into the Healer, and out of the palms of their hands towards the horse. The energy will then find its own way into the physical and energetic parts that it needs to reach. Spiritual Healing can also be carried out at distance in much the same way.

A more commonly known form of Hands on Healing is known as 'Reiki'. It is believed that the ability to heal or channel healing energies is passed down from 'Master' to student through a series of 'attunements'. This of course alone does not make up for experience. It is advised that those who choose this path, continue to learn about healing and the energy systems as a way of gaining as much understanding of it as they can.

## Flower Remedies

Flower remedies are made by infusing wild flowers in spring or mineral water. Brandy is then added as a preservative. The flower infusion then imprints the remedy with the vibration of the flower. This can then be used to correct emotional imbalances. There are literally hundreds of flower remedies available -

each suited to a different state of mind. The most commonly known are the Bach Flower Remedies.

## Radionics

This therapy is sometimes used with what is termed 'The Black Box', or at other times it is used with dowsing. The idea is that the horses' energy systems are read and deciphered, and any blockages or abnormalities are dealt with by sending the correct vibration signature out to them. This therapy in past years was given little credit but more recently, it has become much more widely accepted. As with many other therapies, it can be used not only for correcting health problems, but also with maintaining good health as a preventative. In recent years it has become commonly used in the competition horse world.

## Behaviour Problems

A horse showing the signs of a behaviour problem can be viewed in two different ways: Either as a horse that *is* a problem, or a horse that *has* a problem that chooses to display that it is feeling unsettled. The latter being closer to the truth as an horse is unable to voice its concerns or problems in any other form. The negative feelings being experienced tend to manifest in behaviour that we see as undesirable.

## Possible Symptoms

*Biting*

*Rearing*

*Bucking*

*Chewing (Themselves or others or wood)*

*Not coming when called*

*Kicking or striking*

*Weaving (Swaying the head from side to side whilst stepping from one foot to another)*

*Wind sucking (Gulping in air through the mouth)*

There are many devices on the market making all sorts of claims to stop such behaviours. But is this really the right way of going about it?

*Is it in the best interests of the horse?*

Some of the behaviours listed above release endorphins from the brain that can help to calm the horse. By forcibly stopping such behaviours and not replacing them with something positive or a sense of calmness, we can put our horse's mental well-being under further stress. By removing undesirable behavior, we are not removing the reason for it, so it maybe that over time the horse could start to display another behaviour to replace it. Due to the fact that their original problem is still there and the associated feelings are continuing to be experienced.

By getting to the cause of why the horse feels the need to display such behavior, we can help them address their emotional, environmental and pain related issues to help aid them in disposing of a behaviour that is no longer serving them.

When problems are not addressed or are addressed but in the wrong way, behaviours are open to becoming worse - sometimes even dangerous. By stifling the issue we are in danger of creating another problem, or even causing the horse partial or even full mental breakdown.

The behaviour can escalate to the point that the horse is a real danger to itself and others and completely beyond safe control.

They may retreat into their own world as a way of avoiding total mental collapse. They may even display mental illnesses, such as self-induced Autism or trance states. In either case, the animal will become ungrounded and have little awareness of 'self' - it will reside in its own world. Some horses will give the appearance of going through all the correct physical steps whilst not being completely 'present'. They may stop showing any form of emotion and their negative display of behaviour in certain cases may stop. Unfortunately, when these behaviours stop, and the horse appears quieter and more at rest. It can give the less experienced observer the view that the horse is feeling better when in actual fact, the horse has mentally and emotionally shut down to the point of being almost robotic like - due to the lack of being able to 'feel'.

## Multiple Personality Syndrome

This can easily be recognised in horses by differing kinds of sudden behaviour changes that is often referred to as a 'Jackal and Hyde' type personality. It would appear that Multiple Personality Syndrome in the case of horses, could fall into two categories:

## Dis-Integration

Meaning that the horse's personality has become fragmented. Usually attributed to emotional trauma or faulty chemical systems within the physical body. In human cases of MPS, it has been found that fluctuations in bio-chemicals and neuropeptides can lead to such disorders. There appears to be no logical reason why such fluctuations in these chemicals could not cause the same types of mental illness in horses. However, there is very little if any research carried out on this subject. In the case of severe emotional trauma, it is possible for a horse to invent one or more new personas. These personalities not only appear to have a mind of their own, but usually will have a whole past history of that individual's life.

In a recent communication case that I worked on, the horse in question communicated using three different personalities in quick succession – over the space of around six minutes.

It has been noted in the case of human MPS that not only does the person take on a new identity whilst the secondary (or third as the case maybe) personality is dominant, but the physical body may also take on that personalities illnesses or allergies. It should be noted however, that these illnesses and allergies are only present when the related personality is in place. They can disappear as quickly as they came.

This can cause problems sometimes - for example:

If one personality is allergic to a certain food substance it can be avoided whilst the associated personality is present. However, if the food allergen is still in digestive transit within the body when the allergy prone personality is present - this can then lead to an allergic reaction.

## Outside Influence

Experiments carried out have already shown us that the mind or 'psyche', as it is sometimes referred to, is separate and not directly connected to the brain or the physical body. It has been shown that the mind is able to enter or leave the physical body by choice – free will. This is often the case in horses presenting mental illnesses such as self-induced Autism and trance like states. Though a horse that has these types of mental illnesses, will not automatically also suffer from MPS.

It is not uncommon for another consciousness to make its home in the horse's physical body. In such cases it is often possible to have the 'bogus' personality removed from the horse. This should be carried out by someone who is suitably experienced in these types of cases. When this is carried out correctly, the unwanted behaviour will slowly diminish. It should be noted that this could take time, as the behaviour may have become habitual if the problem has been going on for a while.

## Recognising MPS Through Communication

As our communication with a horse works through our intention to connect with their mind. We can choose to communicate with whatever consciousness, or part of the horse's consciousness, is choosing to exhibit the behaviour.

In the same why as we intend to connect with a certain horse, we can intend to connect to the consciousness responsible for the behavior(s). When we do this, we may find that we feel like we are communicating with a totally different personality altogether. The voice that we hear may soften or come across as harsh, much stronger and more forceful, it may even change gender in style.

Once we have connected to this personality, we can ask them who they are and what their intentions are. This can give us insight as to what is going on if the primary horse personality is unable to clarify the situation, or is unaware of it.

It has been claimed in human cases of MPS that the primary personality has no knowledge of the secondary personality. However, in cases of equine MPS there are some horses that are indeed aware of their other personalities. Though it tends to be more in cases of external personalities rather than fragmentation of the primary.

**The Horses' Environment**

The horses' environment plays a huge role in their physical and emotional well-being. This can encompass all manner of things from basic physical needs such as: Food - to mental stimulation and love. When something is not right within the environment where the horse spends most of its time, it can lead to physical and emotional distress.

## Environmental Needs

*Company*

*Correct diet*

*Suitable shelter*

*Regular exercise*

*Appropriate veterinary care*

*Discipline and training*

*Clean living environment*

*An understanding of where they fit within the 'family' or pecking order*

*Love and physical contact*

## The Owners Influence

As many of our horses spend a lot of their time in our company rather than with their own species, it is not at all unusual for them to become humanised.

This could come in the form of:
Behaviour (taking on the role of the 'parents' child)

When we have horses it is very easy to come to love them in a maternal way. This of course is good from the point of view that we care for them and love them. But we must remember that they have their own needs, be they species related or simply the need to be acknowledged as an individual.

By feeding horses our own foods or specially made processed foods, we can take away their natural dietary requirements. Many horse owners who love their horses as if they were their children, choose to spoil them. This may include letting them get away with behaviour that is seen as unreasonable by others (often caused by distress at the situation they find themselves in), whilst making excuses as to why these behaviours are acceptable.

Observations by horse rescue staff have found that horses that are spoilt can be harder to rehabilitate than horses that have been abused. Whilst finding that the hardest horses to rehabilitate are the ones that have been neglected. By neglected - I am referring to horses that have minimal interaction with others, both human and horse, rather than a lack of good food and medical care.

In the wild, most horses will find themselves living within a herd. Within the herds set order there will be a pecking order. Meaning that each individual knows their place within the group they find themselves. Part of helping to keep our horses mentally balanced, is to help them to understand where exactly they fit in within their horse herd, and their human family. The secret of this of course is consistency in training methods and instruction, as well as welcoming them into the environment as a valuable individual member in the correct way.

# WHAT ARE WE REALLY TELLING THEM?

Horses are very open to reading the thoughts of not only other horses, but also those of their owners and other people that come into their environment. What we think or say consciously does not always equate correctly with our subconscious understanding, needs and desires. Whilst we may think we are saying or believing one thing, it may well be the case that deep down we know differently, or believe in something else entirely. This is where the confusion can lie. No matter how much we convince our self of something - our horses will always see our true intentions and thoughts. It may be that we believe we are thinking in a certain way and backing that up with the relevant body language. However, it may be that at the same time we are not fully resonating with our true belief and our correct understanding of the situation. By the mere fact that we are sending out conflicting information subconsciously (and therefore truthfully on that level) we can often consciously misinform our horses as to what we really mean.

This can lead to two different reactions from our horse. Either the horse will react to our true (subconscious) thoughts and act accordingly. Which can lead us to believe that they are not understanding us correctly, or that they are going against our wishes. Or, the horse can become confused by the conflicting information and become disorientated and not know quite what we are asking them to do. By being as honest with ourselves as we can possibly be and learning to accept and recognise our fears when they are present, we can give our horses much clearer information as to what is really going on.

## Example

A lady has a horse on DIY livery: She works long hours and often asks someone else to check and feed her horse for her. As much as she needs the person to enter her horses stable and feed him, she is not happy at having someone in her horses presence when she is not there.

The horse then intimidates the person who comes to feed him, believing that he is guarding his stable as she is telling him that she doesn't want people entering his stable when she isn't there. At the same time the lady honestly believes that she is telling her horse not to intimidate the person who comes to feed him, as she needs the person to do it.

The situation above, when viewed from the outside, could lead us to believe that the horse is showing all the signs of a behaviour problem. In truth, the horse is just carrying out the subconscious thoughts of his owner by trying to protect his stable and himself at her request. He is fully aware of her not wanting people in his stable or near him whilst she is at work – he acts accordingly as requested.

Situations such as these are very common, especially when an element of fear from the horse's owner is being suppressed to the point that they are not even fully aware of it themselves. In these kinds of situations, rather than reprimanding the horse for their behavior. We have to look at our own thoughts and fears and change them accordingly, to enable us to instruct our horses in a way that gives the desired and most favorable outcome all round.

## The Horse as a Healer

Just as many of us have a natural ability to heal and help others - so do horses. It is commonly known of the wonderful results that swimming with dolphins can bring. In more recent years horses have also played a vital role in human healing due to their intuitive and loving nature, as well as them being more readily accessible to the general public.

Within all relationships experienced in our lifetime, there are lessons to be learnt and experiences to be had. So long as we choose to view the positive in all of our experiences, no experience can be seen as truly bad or wasted.

Many horses come into people's lives as Healers and to teach them of self-worth, understanding and even death. It maybe that you set out to find a particular breed of horse, only to find yourself drawn to something completely different. If this happens go with your gut instinct - as chances are the horse you are being drawn to is one that you need learn from and heal with or through. In such cases our 'chosen' horse may come to us in an unusual or obscure way. Such as a pony you hear of that has just arrived at a local rescue that you feel drawn to give a home to, or you may stumble across a advert on a noticeboard when least expected and feel instantly drawn.

Studies have shown the benefits of keeping horses and the happiness they can bring. This can range from children with learning disabilities who progress against the odds once a new horse has come into the family - to people with high blood pressure who gradually manage to maintain an even pressure when in the presence of a much loved pony. This is largely down to the relaxation that takes place due to the release of the chemical Oxytocin. It is often referred to as the 'cuddle hormone', as it is also excreted during and after giving birth by the dam and foal, or mother and baby.

**The Second Heart Chakra**

Whilst working with my horses in 1995, I was shown a chakra that is light green in colour which is present in the flank of many species of animals. Although linked to the animals' energy systems - it is not directly part of these systems. The animals use this chakra whilst giving healing to others as a way of taking on the negative energies of others and transmuting them. For many animals the taking on of this role is very emotional and brings much responsibility. For this reason, the second heart chakra may remain closed in some animals, until such a time comes that they feel comfortable enough both emotionally and physically to take on their job as a Healer.

Under no circumstances should the second heart chakra be opened in a horse or any other animal that is not yet really. To open this chakra prematurely could bring the animal emotional distress.

# ETHICS AND LEGALITIES

With regards to treating an animal in person the law states:

**Protection of Animals Act 1911**

Legally the owner of any animal may give appropriate treatment so long as it is not considered physically invasive.

The veterinary surgery (exemptions) order of 1962
It is illegal for any complementary therapy to be administered to an animal by anyone other than the animal's owner - unless veterinary permission is first granted.

**Please Note:**

Healing is not a replacement for veterinary care and attention. Anyone who allows an animal to suffer through withholding veterinary attention can be prosecuted.

It is illegal for anyone other than a veterinary surgeon to diagnose an animal. However, you may pass on any information that the animal is giving that can then be passed onto the animal's Veterinary Surgeon. This may go a long way in helping their Vet with a medical diagnosis. Even if you find yourself in the situation where the animal is telling directly that it has a certain illness. It is best advised that the symptoms the animal is feeling be passed on, rather than the actual diagnosis. Diagnosis is best left to the medical profession.

Whilst Horse Communication within some peoples understanding falls into the realm of 'psychic'. It is without a doubt a very important role we play with regards to a horse's physical and emotional welfare. In order to be taken seriously we must remember to work from a professional point of view at all times. Knowing our limits and boundaries and working within them.

It is my personal view that the word 'psychic' should for this reason not be linked to horse communication. It can give the wrong impression and even discredit the wonderful work many Communicators are doing.

It must be remembered that not everyone is open to Horse Communication and those who are aware of it, or even those who have not yet encountered it - may fear it. If this is the case by charging in and giving your two pence worth, you might upset or even alienate the horse's owner.

This is of no benefit to the horse whatsoever. We are here to help the horse, not alienate their owner.

In correctly appropriate situations you might feel comfortable enough to explain to people what you do, and that you feel you could help their horse. It is one thing to make the comment, 'What a happy horse you have', and quite another to comment and say 'Your horse is telling me your husband bullies you'. If the owner has stated that they are happy for you to communicate with their horse and would like to hear what they have to say - then all well and good. However, it is inadvisable to push yourself forwards in a way that might upset people.

**The Permission Issue**

People tend to have different views about this issue. With regards to healing, permission is very important and should only be given with the intention of it being for the horse's highest good. The reason being that by healing a certain emotional problem or physical issue that they have - we may well be taking away their ability to deal with it or heal it themselves which, in some cases needed for their own learning and understanding.

On the communication front do we need the horse's permission? Logic would say that if a horse doesn't want to talk to us then we can't make them. Due to this many would see this as a clearly given answer. After all, we do not ask for permission to speak to someone before we offer the hand of conversation to them. If they don't want to speak to us then they just don't!

However, where do we stand on communicating with someone else's horse when they haven't given their permission, or have openly asked us not to? In these circumstances it very much comes down to how you feel about it and what you are willing or not willing to do. Firstly, we can question whether we need the owner's permission at all? As surely we do not need permission to speak with another living being from someone else? This decision should be left entirely up to the animal? An owner's refusal to allow you to communicate with their horse might be through fear of Horse Communication and not fully understanding it, or stem from a concern that their beloved horse may give away their darkest secrets.

Whether or not you choose to communicate with a horse under these circumstances is very much a personal choice, but the free will of the horse should always be taken into consideration. It might just be that by communicating with the horse you will be helping them a great deal emotionally.

## When People Don't Like What They Hear

There is always the possibility that a horse's owner isn't comfortable with what it is you are telling them. If what you are giving the horse's owner is an answer stemming from a question they have asked you to query their horse about, then logic would say that they should be open to hearing that answer. However, answers aren't always happily accepted. In these cases you have done your job correctly and carried out what you have been asked to do. If the client has an issue with the answer, then this is in no way down to you and it is for them to work through.

If a horse volunteers information of a personal nature about the owner or owner's family. Then it is advisable to ask the client first if they are open to hearing it. This way you are not leaving yourself open to over stepping the mark and causing upset.

**The Sceptic's Challenge**

You will always come across people who are sceptical of things like Horse Communication. They want to catch you out and test you at every opportunity. Ultimately there is only one person who you have to convince of your true ability and that is you. Over time, you will come across people who say, 'If you can't tell me who my horse's best friend is then you can't do it'. Ride over such comments and let them go as this just goes to show the lack of knowledge and understanding of that individual. To try and convince a true sceptic is a very hard thing to do. With most of them no amount of accurate information will convince them. With many of them the bottom line is that they don't want to believe in the existence of Horse Communication - so never will. Your job isn't to convince people of its existence. Your job is to help the horses that are brought to you.

When faced with a sceptic's challenge, just politely tell them that you are busy and maybe recommend some books on Animal Communication that they might like to read. In giving you this challenge they are simply wanting to see your downfall so they can say 'I told you so'. When we are put in such situations our stress levels will rise and straight away we make things much harder for ourselves. For these reasons it would be advisable to steer clear of such situations as there is no reason at all for you to be challenged by anyone.

# TRACKING LOST AND STOLEN HORSES

It is a sad fact that every year in the UK many horses are stolen. Tracking a lost or stolen horse can put a Communicator under a huge amount of pressure for several reasons:

*The pressure put on themselves in wanting to help so much.*

*The horse maybe on the move.*

*If the horse is very distressed - it may have trouble communicating.*

*You may pick up on the residual energy of where they have been, rather than where they are.*

*If you work with Animal Guides you may want to ask them for any input or insights that they may have.*

*Start by communicating with the animal in the way that you normally would.*

## Suggested Questions

*Do they feel safe?*

*Are they injured?*

*Are they hungry?*

*What do they see around them?*

*Do they know where they are?*

*Have they been taken in by someone?*

*Did they leave of their own accord or were they taken?*

*Do they know why it happened?*

As well as asking questions, we can also work with something known as 'remote viewing'. This involves astrally projecting (leaving the body) and going to where the horse is. This can be done during meditation. We can then imagine being in the air above the horse, watching them and their surrounds. By doing this we may see landmarks or even signposts with names on.

Alternatively, we can ask a horse to show us what they are seeing through their eyes. When this happens you may find yourself watching what looks like a film.

Tracking missing horses is always hard and can be very hit and miss. Don't be disheartened if you are unable to help to locate a horse. As it may be the next one you are asked to work with is found safe and sound.

# The Energetic Dynamics Behind The Disappearance

As with everything, an energetic blueprint is made in order that the physical reality can then manifest. Through meditation we can imagine the missing horse behind a closed door, the other side of the door being the horse's way home. We can then step through the door to see what is the other side of it and is stopping the horse from entering through the door and returning home. By removing such obstacles we can help to alter the energetic dynamic and hopefully help the horse to be found.

## The Horses' Life Path

All horses have a destined path to walk in much the same way as we do. Life is free will for horses, but they often feel obliged to live the way we want them to. Due to them often finding themselves in unfavorable circumstances, they are sometimes unable to complete what they came here to do. We have already previously discussed how 'chosen' horses may come to us under strange circumstances. When we don't listen to our intuition and follow what we need to do, not only are we affecting our own destiny, but also that of the horse involved.

## Karma

Karma is created when we wrong someone or they do something to us that they shouldn't. When this happens we create what is known as a 'Karmic debt' towards that person or animal. Sooner or later that debt will need to be paid back. It maybe that the horse or person who we need to work the debt through with, comes into contact with us in this life time, or the debt may be carried over to the next life time. Until the debt is paid, the cycle will be on going. This is where the phases, 'What goes around comes around' and 'You reap what you sow' come from.

It maybe that within the relationship with your horse(s), all karmic debts have been cleared in past lifetimes, or that there were never any such debts to be paid. It could be that your horse found their way to you. As you were the right person to put them in the position to enable them to complete their life's lesson or task this time around.

## Examples

*To enable them to fulfill their role as a Healer.*

*To help them pass on important information to help either yourself or others.*

*So that they can be close to another person or animal to work through a karmic debt.*

*You might be an intermediate stop for them finding the person they are meant to be with.*

*To enable them to become physically or emotionally well so they may continue their work.*

*Whatever the reason for your horse finding their way to you, in time you will come to understand it and help them progress spiritually and fulfill their life's purpose.*

As with all living things, there will come a time when the horse is ready to leave the physical plane. Obviously the more pain free and quieter this is for them the better. Animals view death a little differently from most people, in as much as they see it as just another part of the ongoing cycle of life. Though of course, that is not to say that some aren't desperate to stay with their friends and those they view as family. They have an acceptance of death and don't fear it as we do. When we come to accept this, we make it far easier for our much-loved family horses to leave us when their time has come. When a horse is elderly and is in pain, or when our horse has been unwell for a long time with no chance of recovery, why mourn their death when we can rejoice in their life and the memories we shared?

*Who are we crying for - the horse who has returned home, or for our self?*

To love a horse one 100% is to let them go when their time has come. To hold them close and tell them that it's all right for them to go. That we love them and we wish them well. To then close our eyes and imagine the energetic cords that connect you to them. Visualise yourself cutting them with love whilst watching them slowly float away. This is the action of true love. Think of the good times and the lessons learnt and you will see that their life was never wasted. Death can be beautiful when we can see the bigger picture and interpret it as such – all too often healing comes through death.

It may even be that you find yourself taking in all kinds of horses and ponies and that despite your best efforts, you are unable to make them well. Maybe you just happen to be the right person they can feel safe with so that they feel they can go. Maybe that is your part to play in their healing - their release.

So many people I meet feel guilty about their horse's illness or passing. they feel that they didn't do enough to help them in their hour of need. When I meet people who have these thoughts I ask them: 'Did you do everything you were mentally and physically capable of doing?' More often than not the answer is 'yes'. I then gently explain to them that this being the case, they have done nothing wrong. Sometimes to hear this from another person is enough to reverse years of guilt, though of course nothing can be as wonderful as hearing this information from their horse themselves.

*True love doesn't blame, hold resentment or ever die.*
*It is eternal.*

## Past-Life Memories and Injures

It is not at all unusual for horses to talk about other life times they have experienced, even lives as a human. Some people still view animals as their underlings and have a hard time acknowledging that animals have had lives as humans. As your communication skills progress and your mind expands and accepts new possibilities, this understanding will become perfectly acceptable to you.

## Past-life information may come in several ways:

*The horse may show you images of themselves in another body.*

*The horse may talk about 'when I was....'*

*They might say to you 'When I was with you before....'*

*You may just have a feeling of 'knowing' the horse during your first encounter with them.*

The memories that we hold within our electromagnetic energy field are carried with us from lifetime to lifetime. Within the field our past memories, experiences and energetic disruptions also exist. They accompany us to our present lifetime. When we suffer illnesses or injuries in past lives, we weaken part of the aura. This can make a horse susceptible to new illnesses manifesting in this life time. The emotional traumas experienced in these other life times our held within the subconscious. These can sometimes lead to psychosomatic allergies, phobias and seemingly irrational fears. By working through these fears and traumas and finding out how and why they began, we can start to heal them. Part of the way we can work towards this is by helping the horse to remain in the here and now. Enabling them to understand what was 'then' and what is 'now'. Working energetically with the aura will also help in the mending process.

## Giving Thanks

It should be remembered at all times that horses don't have to speak to us. Nor do they need to help us - they choose to. At all times this should be appreciated and understood. Always 'thank' a horse for their help and for speaking with you, as often a 'thank you' goes a long way. Asking them if there is anything you can do for them is always a nice way to repay the favor.

# CHOOSE YOUR TITLE CAREFULLY

*What is actually in a title?*

*What is the purpose?*

*Why is it so important?*

Our title tells people who we are and what we do. When we do not give ourselves a correct title it can cause people to misunderstand what we do and what we are about. I tend to use the title 'Animal Communicator' or 'Horse Communicator', as this is what I do and who I am. It is my role and vocation in life and an innate part of who I am. Quite simply put: my career is one of communicating with horses and helping them to be heard, as well as helping their human Guardians too.

Sadly there are labels that are being used that are not necessarily in the best interests of our work and for explaining what it is that we do. These are titles such as Horse Psychic and Horse Medium. I must admit that these titles make me cringe. The reason being, that they can bring about the dial a psychic for £1.50 a minute ideas to mind. The 'spooky ' your horse has a white spot on his bum' Communicators, whose client exclaim they are 'correct' and 'wow'. Is this really what we are and how we want to be viewed?

Further more: Is this actually productive for horse? Let's face it, the horse with a white spot on his bum knows he has a white spot as does his Guardian. So what actually is gained in such a communication and the passing on of this information? The information that needs to be passed on is far more important than that. Imagine living in a foreign country and only being able to speak the native language for an hour of your life. There is far more important information that needs to be heard and passed on, in order to help in the creation of change for the better for that horse.

Further to this, using words such as 'psychic' can also stop us, and the information offered from the horse, from being taken seriously by some individuals. A classically trained Vet is more likely to be open minded and interested to as what the role of an 'Animal Communicator' is and what they do, than he is of an Animal Psychic that he may choose to instantly dismiss as 'hocus pocus' due to title alone.

Whilst it is fair to say that many Animal Communicators are psychic and that many also work as Mediums. Titling yourself as such, or mixing your horse work with Mediumship, can be misleading and bring about the wrong impression. It may even cause a loss of credibility. Not just for yourself, but also for other Animal and Horse Communicators. I have no doubt that some Communicators will be feeling that in saying this I am being a little judgmental.

*But rather than looking at it that way, consider instead how others may view it.*

Including those clients who have horses that are sick, have behaviour problems and are in need of your help. As the reason that I am choosing to explain this, even knowing it may cause offence for some, is to try and help the animal communication movement as a whole. To help aid us in getting the recognition that we rightfully deserve.

For this reason my advice would be to label your self wisely. Instead of taking offence at what I have said, look at the bigger picture. Look at how other people may view you and the kind of clients it may cause you to attract. As well as how it may cause you and others to be viewed.

Animal and Horse Communication are a form of Mediumship, but that does not mean it needs to be associated with 'talking to dead people' and 'I have your grandmother Florence here with the pink hair'.

Your title alone will have a huge effect on how people view not only you, but also others on this chosen path.

I have also come across some Communicators that have chosen to give themselves strange names, rather than using their everyday names. Again this brings to mind the word 'psychic' and can cause people to put you into the 'mystical' category. This is not what we need to be aiming for and though whilst some may find it draws to them the kind of clients they like. It may not be the case that through the type of 'readings' that they are doing, that they are working to the best of their ability. In instances such as these it will only be the horses that suffer and miss out.

*Horse Communication is a serious subject and it needs to be treated as such.*

Recently I put a horse communication consultation up as a prize in a raffle, to help raise money for a horse sanctuary. I was given the name of the person that had won it by the organiser and I emailed her. I asked her for the age, name and gender of her horse. Along with any white face markings and what she would like me to ask her horse about for her. Her reply came back that I would be glad to hear that her mother was one of the best known psychics in England. She said that she thought that I would be pleased as that meant she believed in this kind of psychic connection.

My heart sank - just these three lines alone showed what she thought my role was, and that she thought me a psychic that 'reads' horses for entertainment. Her comment that it was good news to me as it meant she believed in this kind of psychic connection, just went to further show me that she was a 'tester' and was not fully understanding my work - its importance and my role in helping them both.

She also asked me, could she not divulge any information and that I just 'read' her horse to see what I got. I politely messaged her back explaining that I am not a psychic and my connection is a direct connection with the horse. My reasoning for asking for questions is that all horses are different. Some are chatty and have open personalities - whilst some are not so, so it is always good to have some questions handy. As a way of starting off conversation and that it also enables the Guardian to find out about what they need to - based on their concerns. Not only this, but this is the way that I have been working in my profession all of these years. That I consider myself an Animal Communicator and Therapist and not a Psychic that does readings for entertainment.

I was told then that the 'prize' should be re-raffled as it was no use to her, as there was nothing wrong with her horse. That reply I felt was a bit of a shame. This lady did not know whether or not her horse may have a virus that showed no external symptoms that may have been sat there for years knocking the immune system. She did not know if her horse was lame, as it may have been experiencing a masked pain, so that he did not present as lame visually, or had multiple lameness.

Her total dismissing of the communication was because she expected me to be a psychic reader, whose job was telling people things about their horses that they already knew. What is the point in that? To take and use it as some sort of entertainment, dependent on whether it fit in with what she thought about her horse or not. This is not and will never be the kind of person I wish to work for. Nor is this a positive way of helping horses.

*What is the point?*

When someone is this closed minded as to think there is nothing wrong with their horse? In all my years of animal communication which has clocked up literally thousands of communications with horses. The least number if physical issues I have ever found in any one horse is three. This was a three year old horse that belonged to an Equine Physiotherapist. This lady had not even stopped to consider that her horse had feelings, may need his voice heard and had issues that she was unaware of.

It is totally understandable that there are sceptics out there. I personally feel that until someone fully experiences or learns about it, then a degree of open minded scepticism is healthy. I have come across too many clients that are all too willing to pay any amount and believe anything they are told that it concerns me. There have even been times that I have pulled clients to one side and gently explained to them that, there are charlatans out there and not everyone loves horses and wants to help in the way they profess they want to.

Another common title used by Horse Communicators is 'Horse Whisper'. Again this title can be misleading. 'Whispering' refers to the observation and assessment of the horses' body language. It is not the same connection that we use in horse communication. 'Whispers' tend to work more with training horses and engaging with them by reading the subtle cues that they are displaying physically through their expression and movement. This should not be confused with the telepathic connection that Horse Communicators have with horses. That said, many Horse Communicators also choose to work with Whispering in addition to their horse communication work. These two ways of communicating with horses work well together. Even though there are obvious difference between the two types of approach and the dynamics involved.

# ARE HORSES PYSCHIC OR INTUITIVE?

*Which would you consider yourself to be?*

*Do you 'read' the horse, or do you have a direct line of communication with them?*

*Do you consider yourself 'psychic' and what does psychic even mean?*

"'Relating to or denoting faculties or phenomena that are apparently inexplicable by natural laws".

"Psychic powers"

**Words associated with psychic:**

*Supernatural, paranormal, other-worldly, supernormal, preternatural, metaphysical, extrasensory, transcendental, magic, magical, mystical, mystic and occult.*

There is nothing paranormal about horse communication any more than there is anything mystical about it. Horse communication is simply a natural sense and ability that we all have and that is innate to us. It simply enables us to mentally travel and connect to and with the horse on a subtle level. Enabling us to decipher the subtle information and knowledge that exists within them and that they are aware of.

Yes, the experience may feel mystical, transcendental and magical, but this is all just part of how we relate to it and how it feels to us. The connection of two energies is simple physics and natural. It is an innate ability that we all have and to a large degree as humans, deny not only to ourselves, but by consequence to the animal kingdom as well.

### Now let us look at the word "Intuitive".

Intuitive meaning - based on what one feels to be true even without conscious reasoning; instinctive.

### Words associated with the word "intuitive".

*Instinctive, intuitional and instinctual.*

*Now do those meanings in reference to horse communication sit more comfortably to you?*

When we communicate with a horse. It is not just about what we hear - but also what we *feel* that is important. This may come as gut intuition, or just a 'knowing' that what we are hearing is correct, or that it just does not feel right. This then may cause us to start to question down another line of enquiry, that will bring about an outcome that has aided the horse and their Guardian.

It is not just about what we hear, it is also about gathering together and working through all of the additional information that comes with it.

Psychic and intuitive are very different and one should not become confused with the other. Whilst it is fair to say that most Communicators will work with both psychic ability and intuition. I feel it is safe to say that the most forth coming and important communications will come through our intuitive abilities and our rational ones.

'Reading' a horse is very different to 'direct connection' with them. The reading of a horse is a third party opinion of that horse, if the information is being 'given' and 'offered' to you by another source. If you are reading the horse yourself, there is no problem with this at all, so long as you are reading them correctly. I just feel that it is important to understand the difference between reading and direct communication. As strictly speaking the reading of a horse, is not really horse communication.

Direct communication with horses enables us to ask questions and hear information from them first hand. What we should also be aware of too, is that what we choose to hear is the horse's own version of the story - as they saw and experienced it. What one individual may see and experience in one way - may be very different from the next horse's personal experience, or even how the Guardian has experienced and felt about it. For this reason it is always important to bear in mind that the opinion of the horse may be biased when they are choosing to speak out for all of their species. It may be that they are only be speaking on behalf of certain individuals within that species as well as themselves, without being aware of that fact. Some may have different feelings about an event, experience, their species or situation entirely.

*So are horses psychic?*

Yes and no - it depends very much on how the horse (the same as a person) directs their energy towards others and deciphers another's energy. A horse that can sniff out cancer or detect the early onset of a seizure is not psychic. He is simply picking up on the electromagnetic changes of the body's energy, the change in brain wave pattern (if this should be the case) and the change in the chemicals in the person or animal's body through his olfactory system. There is nothing remotely psychic about that. It is just all part of the innate sense that the horse uses, that to a large degree has been lost by humans.

Some Communicators will tell stories of horses that have foretold the future and been correct. So should be consider this psychic? Well indeed it may fall into those realms and the description of its meaning.

Let us not forget what the horse truly is. They are a soul, a consciousness with a physical body that enables them (like us) to live out an earthy experience and evolve and hopefully progress. If the assumption holds true that we journey through many life times, then it would also stand to reason that those events, experiences and memories of other life times, would be held still within that consciousness. This taken into consideration then no - it is not of any wonder that horses can speak the way they do about having lived through other life times. As well as their relaying of information that you would not have expected them to be able to other wise gain.

The moment we connect with a horse they are able to see and read our thoughts and intentions. Due to this, they are often able to understand things such as different therapies for example, that they may well not have experienced first-hand.

There are many things that science has yet to understand, research and prove. Science will only ever be as good and keeping up with the times, as will those that are within the scientific field.

# WHY ASK FOR QUESTIONS

Like people, horses will all have their own unique personalities. Some will be more 'chatty' and forth coming than others, whilst some choose to hold back when in the presence of new company, or any company other than a few close friends. Due to this, it is always wise to have some questions handy from the horse's Guardian.

This will also enable you to know how best to direct the communication, from the point of view of what information is being looked for. If for instance the horse is in pain, and that pain is long standing. They may not choose to mention it as it has become part of everyday life for them. They may have developed a high pain threshold and just 'deal with it' and accept it on a daily basis. The horse may also be aware that the Guardian knows about the pain. Due to this, in an open communication where questions are not asked, the horse may not even mention it.

This is one of the many reasons why questions are so important. It also may be that an issue or problem that the horse has, they may feel is not able to be sorted. Again due to this, it may be something that they then choose not to bother voicing unless asked.

Without asking the relevant questions, we may end up just throwing up random pieces of information. In the long run this is of little use to the horse and their Guardian. By working on a question and answer type basis, it will not only help with horses that feel they have little to say, but also means that what is needed to be voiced and brought to light can be.

Another example of this is in cases where the horse has a degenerative issue with their sight or hearing. The degeneration may have been slow so that they may not have really noticed it much. Due to this, they may not choose to voice that they have an issue with one or either, as they are not actually aware of it themselves. Through asking them about it, it causes them to focus on it in a way that may bring it to light. Another way that we can also access issues such as these. Is to ask the horse to allow us to see through their eyes and hear through their ears as they do. By doing this we can see and hear if there is any difference between the two ears or eyes and any loss or distortion.

# ASSESSING PAIN LEVELS

This is a subject that a lot of Horse Communicators tell me that they struggle with. Just how do you assess pain levels in someone else, or a horse other than by physical observation and heart rate?

I have found that the easily way to go about this is to use a score chart. I use zero to mean no pain is being experienced in that area and ten to mean unbearable pain. I then ask the horse to give me a figure based on over-all average pain and another figure for when the pain is at its worst.

Bear in mind too, that issues such as arthritis may change in their pain levels, dependent on the time of year. They may get worse during seasons that have a lot of cold and damp weather. Intermittent and sharp, sudden pains also may score differently at different times.

We also need to take into consideration the difference between observation of physically presenting symptoms, and each individual's pain threshold. If the horse has long term pain that they have had to live with. Chances are they are used to it to a degree and that the symptoms may not present themselves visually, in the same way that they would do in cases of acute pain. Whilst one horse may still be walking on a lame leg, another horse in equally as much pain, may choose not to weight bare at all.

Some horses will have been prescribed pain relief by their Veterinary Surgeon. This may be for acute or chronic issues. In the case of chronic issues I always advise my client's to also look into additional and alternative types of pain relief. This may come in the form of aromatics, homeopathy or therapies, that will further help with pain management rather than just going down the drug route alone.

Horses can suffer unbearable pain and yet at the same time not obviously physically present it. There are several symptoms that should be looked out for that are also a good indicator as to the levels being experienced.

*Head pressing against walls or other flat objects*

*Head banging*

*Unusually immobile and choosing not to move around much*

*Lack of sleep*

*A change in behaviour such as having little tolerance and becoming easily frustrated*

*Violent behaviour or outbursts that are out of character for the individual*

*Refusing to eat their everyday food or taking an abnormal lack of interest in it*

*A usually willing horse not wanting to be ridden*

*Tightness in the muscles around the eyes and mouth*

*Ears back when resting (but not due to listening) and an overall non relaxed facial expression*

If the horse is in pain, it is important to stress to the horse's Guardian that action needs to be taken in the form of some kind of medical intervention, to try and stop further suffering immediately. There are also many other avenues that then can be additionally explored to aid the horse further.

If a client's horse is in pain, they need to see a qualified Veterinary Surgeon for assessment and treatment.

# THE FINE LINE OF DIAGNOSING

So what is diagnosing and where is the line drawn?

If we see a horse hopping on three legs and holding up its forth leg due to pain and we say, 'that horse is lame' - are we then diagnosing? If so, then most people that work with, or have horses in their daily lives are breaking the law on a regular basis - according to the Veterinary Surgeons Act 19.2 (a).

**When it comes to diagnosis the Veterinary Surgeons Act 1996 states:**

19.1 The purpose of this guidance is to explain the restrictions that apply under the Veterinary Surgeons Act 1966 ('the Act') to ensure that animals are treated only by those people qualified to do so. These restrictions apply where the 'treatment' is considered to be the practice of 'veterinary surgery', as defined by the Act.

19.2 Section 19 of the Act provides, subject to a number of exceptions, that only registered members of the Royal College of Veterinary Surgeons may practise veterinary surgery. 'Veterinary surgery' is defined within the Act as follows:

'Veterinary Surgery means the art and science of veterinary surgery and medicine and, without prejudice to the generality of the foregoing, shall be taken to include -

a. the diagnosis of diseases in, and injuries to, animals including tests performed on animals for diagnostic purposes;

b. the giving of advice based upon such diagnosis;

c. the medical or surgical treatment of animals; and

d. the performance of surgical operations on animals.'

The Veterinary Surgeons Act is a double edged sword. Whilst it aims to protect animals from charlatans and safe guard their physical welfare. It also limits the ability of certain qualified individuals that are excellent in their chosen field and career, in their ability to help animals in need. This can be seen all too easily by the handful of Veterinary Surgeons that choose to not give their permission for other professionals such as Osteopaths and Chiropractors to assess and treat some horses. Even in the absence of them themselves being able to provide a valid diagnosis and treatment.

*So where do Horse Communicators stand?*

There is a fine line in regards to diagnosing as already discussed. When we pass on information from the horse are we actually diagnosing? If the horse is telling us about their symptoms and we are relaying that information to the horse's Guardian, or their Veterinary Surgeon. How exactly are we diagnosing? We are not looking at the horse physically and making a clinical diagnosis based on our own findings. In the case of body scanning we are passing in information relating to energetic disruptions found - not physical ones. Maybe aided by the information also given to us by the horse in question that is having the actual experience.

Whether or not the Veterinary Surgeon or Guardian choose to take this information up, is beyond our control. But for the horse's sake, if this information has been offered by them, the one that is in fact experiencing those symptoms - surely it in within our duty to pass that information on?

Any medical issues that do come to light should be voiced to the horse's Guardian. With the advice that they seek medical advice from their Vet for it. They can also choose to research alternatives and things that are additional and may help. First point of call should be, and needs to be their Veterinary Surgeon. They are suitably qualified and have the knowledge needed, and apparatus available, to make a proper and informed clinical diagnosis which is much needed.

Horse communication in cases of health issues, is in addition to correct care from the horse's Veterinary Surgeon. It is not, and should not, be considered a replacement for it.

That said, every week I come across clients that have horse's, for which their Veterinary Surgeons have not been able to give a firm medical diagnosis. Without such a diagnosis it makes it hard to give a prognosis and a course of correct treatment. On-going lameness issues and general lethargy are often the cases that I come across. It is not unusual for horses to have a lingering virus that continually knocks their immune system. Whilst providing no external symptoms other than fatigue. This can easily be over looked by Guardians and titled 'laziness' on the part of the horse. Further to this, these types of virus may lead to infection, again with no obvious external symptoms and then also snowball into anaemia.

*A tired and lethargic horse is one that has a problem that needs looking into.*

This is why something as simple as fatigue should always be taken extremely seriously, as it may also indicate severe pain issues. It is hard for a Vet to make a diagnosis when no obvious symptoms are presenting themselves. Due to the horse's Guardian being used to their normal behaviour. Any slight divination from that, may well be seen and taken as a vital sign that something is wrong with them. Once presented for clinical examination it is then not uncommon for horses to be given the all clear, due to a lack of symptoms. This is where Horse Communication can be invaluable. It enables the horse to be able to pass on felt - but not physically presenting symptoms.

## Some examples of these will be:

*Feeling sick, but without physically vomiting (due to their anatomy horses can't be physically sick, but that does not prevent them from feeling sick)*

*Severe fatigue (an active horse may slow down only a little and feel much more tired and drained than it physically presents)*

*Lameness that does not become more painful upon weight baring, so the horse may not physically present as being lame. Pain in the chest and a tickling sensation that may not present as a cough*

*Skin sensitivity and damaged nerve endings that may not feel worse when touched*

*Nerve damage or pain that may be diagnosed as a lack of correct movement due to lack of schooling.*

Several years ago I went out to my stable yard to find my little Welsh pony sweating - his whole body stank. He was stood in a laminitic stance and was shaking. When only a few hours earlier, he had been presenting no symptoms at all. I called the Vet immediately, who then turned up an hour later. He injected the pony with Buscopan and then expected to leave. I stood my ground - pointed out his symptoms and told the Vet that I believed him to have an internal infection and an issue with his liver - based on his presenting symptoms. I then demanded that he be blood tested and be given antibiotics as well. The blood results came back the following morning. They showed that he had an infection and hepatitis.

My pony when I found him - was so sick, and his illness had come on so rapidly, that I had also asked to have him referred to the local hospital. I was told that my pony was not sick enough to go to hospital in a Sunday evening. How can any Vet state this when they have not even given a diagnosis? My pony was barely able to stand. He very obviously had a serious issue with his liver based upon the very strong smell coming from his body, that had manifested in a matter of a few hours. In fact, he was actually dying - he was that seriously ill. After eight long weeks on box rest (we had been having hard frost and snow so it was also not safe to let him out due to that, in light of his laminitis) he was able to be turned back out.

He went through the summer easily, but as soon as the first frost came the following autumn, he came down with laminitis. This was even though I stabled him for the night and went out at 11pm to give him warm water to drink. His sweat patches had also reappeared - so we had to call it a day for his sake, as he was so internally sick. This just goes to show how sick he had been that winter and the damage caused by his illness. I have no doubt that had I not have stepped in with a diagnosis for him and demanded his correct treatment - he would have been dead by morning.

Needless to say I reported the Vet involved to the RCVS. Sadly he was let off due to his report on the visit being very different from my own truthful and correct one.

Just because someone has letters after their name or is trained and qualified in their chosen career, it does not mean integrity reins. Nor does it mean they even care about horses. For some people no matter what their career in life, it is just that - a career. Anyone in a career within the care sector is open to falling prey to becoming mechanical and un-compassionate. Do not fall prey to allowing your heart and mind to close where the horses are concerned.

If you do not have knowledge in the physiology and the working of the bodies of horses. Then my advice is to stay away from such cases. Instead, refer on to those that specialise in those areas.

We should, and must, be aiming to work with Veterinary Surgeons - not against them. We are all only human and can only do the best that we can (when and if we choose to, which sadly is not always the case). Finding and working with an open minded and willing Veterinary Surgeon, can go a long way to help horses in need and in forming a good team to enable that to happen.

There are good and bad in all careers, or rather those that truly care and those that do not. It is not about the career, so much as the individual that is in that career. Needless to say, there is an alternative meaning to 'practising' in any career - rather than actually doing it.

# THE SELECTIVE COMMUNICATOR

How we choose to 'hear' horses and indeed 'how' we hear them, will be through personal choice and in some cases, due to our lack of knowledge and our own biased way of thinking.

If we are closed minded and have a rigid way of thinking - meaning that when we have an opinion on something, we are not flexible to the fact what is right for one may be wrong for the next. Either through our lack of understanding that there are other ways and options, or that we do not know that those exist. We will limit our abilities within our communication skills. This will have a profoundly biased outcome to how we both hear and feel the horse express them-self.

An example of this is if we are fascinated with just one training method or therapy - think it the best thing since sliced bread and nothing can even measure up to it - we then tunnel vision ourselves. We will never allow ourselves to hear the horse state that this is the incorrect (or not the best) method to be used for them. Sadly I have seen this happen again and again, whereby Communicators advocate the same training method be used for each individual horse. The difference in personalities and needs (need being survival and want being desire) of the individual not being taken into consideration, so the best outcome therefore is not achieved. In some cases even disaster occurring. Therapists and Trainers as well as Medical Professionals in many cases are also guilty of this.

Rather, it is of utmost importance to understand that what is truth for us, may not be for the next. Growth is about learning, exploration, education and personal experience. Within this will be found and produced the art of the unbiased and open mind. The same mind that rejects selectism on what is heard, repeated and offered to the horse's Guardian.

Sadly an open mind can't be taught; it is innate and based on experience, life path and individuality as well as personal perception. It is the art of being analytical and maintaining a quiet and well trained mind. Not conditioned - but well organised and with all information relating to others being carefully filed, to enable it to be found as and when needed.

For those truth seekers - the open minded folk - life will be a lot easier. These individuals will find themselves rarely offended by what others say. They are constantly questioning the 'why' in everything and are only to open to the fact that they may be wrong. The ones that can put their hands up and say 'I could have done that better so what has it taught me, so I can do better next time around?' Understanding that each day holds lessons and knowledge with each interaction and thought. These are the explorers and seekers in life and those that will in most cases, if compassion exists within them also, will likely make the best Communicators and Facilitators.

If giving horses their true voice to the best of our ability is what we consider our role to be. Then without a doubt we owe it not just to them, but also ourselves, to get our own mind in order and our life in order to enable us to be as balanced and unbiased as possible. Not an easy task for some - but possible for those that truly seek it.

Often it is not the destination that is important on our personal journey's, but also the route that we choose to take to reach that destination and what we learn about ourselves on the way. This is the point at which positive change can be made and created and the magical mind is enabled to flourish.

# AUTISM, LEARNING DIFFICULTIES AND DEMENTIA

Horses have all of the same Neuro-Peptides (emotional brain chemicals) that humans do. Not only are these emotional chemicals found in the brain, but also in the gut (Hence the term gut reaction and gut feeling, as well as stomach upset or sensation due to stress or excitement).

The mind of any individual, along with their consciousness and extremely vast and in depth nature, will have a profound effect on how they think, feel and their perception. Not forgetting the biological functioning and if you like 'wiring' of each brain that enables us all to be individuals.

Due to this as with people, horses can and do suffer from all of the same emotional and psychological issues that we do.

Over the years it has been my privilege to work with some such individuals in horse form. From my Arabian Manta that displays Autistic like traits and learning issues - to client's horses suffering with learning issues. (Though I feel it is important to add what we may see as suffering for them may in fact be acceptable and even normal to them – they may never have experienced otherwise, or even know there is an issue. The suffering in fact is sometimes only present when another is unable to meet them and understand them on their own level).

Several years ago a lady contacted me about her horse. He had a history of what at times could be considered violent behaviour. The lady in question was an experienced horse woman, but no matter what she tried, no real improvement was being seen. We chatted and she booked a consultation for her and her horse to talk to me.

To cut a long story short, from a psychological analysis of not just what the horse was 'saying' to me, his behaviour as observed by his Guardian and more importantly, what I felt that he was not saying. I was able to draw the conclusion that he was in fact somewhere on the Autistic Spectrum. I was able to discuss this with his Guardian and also throw around ideas with her on the best approach to take when interacting with him. Due to his Autism, the everyday way best suited to the average individual approach may not suit him. As he was not average in his ability to hear and work things through in the same way another horse would.

His Guardian decided that to be 100% sure of this she would also take the approach of having all of the relevant tests carried out, in order to exclude other causes for his behaviour. Four thousand pounds later the Vet came back with a diagnosis of Autism.

His Guardian had not made the Vet aware of what I suspected until afterwards. As far as I am aware this was and still is, the only actual 'diagnosis' of Autism in a horse in the UK today by a Veterinary Surgeon. There may be others and being as it is so common, I hope there is, but if there is I have yet to hear of them. However, to my way of thinking that one veterinary diagnosis speaks volumes. It shows that 'someone' in the clinical medical professional has accepted it for what it is. I hope it is just the first small step in paving the way forwards for further accepting horses as individuals. Especially within a world in which some in the medical profession still to this day, ignorantly deny the existence of animals having emotions. Even though the biological and scientific evidence of their emotional chemicals and molecules are well proven.

Once again with the utmost respect I would say that if your background is not one of knowledge in psychology and mental health, or is at best 'sketchy'. In instances such as these, if you feel that you are not sure but suspect that there is a psychological issue, or one of mental health that it may fall into one of the above categories. It is best to refer the client on to someone else that is more knowledgeable in that field.

# My little black Manta's issues present in several ways:

*His inability to interact fully and comfortably on a consistent basis with people. This may show its self as one moment looking at you worriedly, as if he does not recognise you - to walking straight up to you with complete confidence and giving you a kiss.*

*A discrepancy in how and where he stores and retrieves information, by way of his long and short term memory.*

*The ability to understand a few training words by association, but not to associate a word with 'himself'. By this I am referring to when we call a horse by name and they acknowledge that association.*

*His slowed or incorrect responses to other equine's cues offered to him. These do improve in a relaxed herd environment such as the one he has living in with my other horses.*

*His ability to slow his heart and breath rate in times a stress and close down and remove himself both mentally and physically, to avoid mental collapse.*

*At times (but not consistent) consistently offering incorrect responses to cues and requests offered, even when he has learnt and correctly responded to the same requests many times before.*

The Autistic Spectrum is as wide as it is long. No two personalities will consistently show and display the same characteristics. This of course can make it all the harder to fully grasp in many cases, if this is indeed the presenting cause of the problem. It is commonly believed that in the case of Autism there is a lack or absence of emotion. In fact nothing could be further from the truth. Usually the resulting behaviour is due to an inability to deal with either their own emotion's and energy, or that of others, in a way that is constructive to them. This inability may at times choose to present itself as a closing down and numbing of those emotions, to stop them being inwardly felt and outwardly expressed. This of course then results in the ability of the individual in being able lower the heart and breath rate as the emotion is not being felt. The opposite end of the scale is the horse that is unable to close themselves down in such a way, as to create emotional safe guard for themselves. Instead overflowing, mentally, energetically and thus physically into the physical explosion that we so often see, due to their inability to cope with their own emotions - those of others, and what is being laid at their door in that moment in time.

Like humans, horses with Autism and learning issues need a bespoke and well considered approach in how we both physically and emotionally communicate with them, as well as their training and interactions with others.

# THE PSYCHLOGICAL SAFETY ZONE

The Psychological Safety Zone exists as much with Horse Communicators and people in general - as it does with horses. Often what is 'known' is 'safe', even if not particularly 'liked'. To give an example of this, I will use my experience of helping out for a day at a primate sanctuary.

For my husband's birthday I paid for us to spend the day as 'helpers' at a Primate Sanctuary. This involved cleaning of their areas and preparing their food, as well as spending quality time with the beautiful primates that lived there. One thing that struck me immediately was the difference in their living environments. One monkey had a large grassy area and was all by himself. There was low fencing, but he chose to stay within it and had plenty of freedom to roam and swing around the posts that were in there for him to use as his activity centre. Yet next to his playground was a small cage run type area that was fully closed in with wire, and housed quite a few smaller primates.

On first observation I wondered why one was given such freedom and was alone and yet others had such a small area and looked 'overcrowded'. It was explained to me by the Animal Psychologist that was accompanying us for the day, that the primate that was alone had previous lived his life without company. He was unable to identify with other primates and when he was in their company, he would bully them. But left to his own devices and given the freedom to play and express, he was neither bored nor stressed. His own little world revolved around his play area, his freedom and his ability to be able to create his own amusement and quality time in a way that suited 'him'. If introduced to others it was concerning to him to have to step out of his safety zone, in a way that he was emotionally unable to deal with.

The small cage run of primates was another story entirely. They had been rescued from a laboratory. Their life had been one of 'enclosure' with little space and with other primates close by. This had been their world and experience for so many years, that they were unable to mentally cope with 'space'. For these little guys enclosure was safe, maybe not liked - but safe. Whilst it took away their freedom to a certain extent, it was also removing the freedom they were mentally unable to cope with. This in mind their confinement was actually 'emotional kindness', that was being offered to them by those that fully understood their needs.

Next we were to visit 'Mo', another little guy that lived alone and liked to spend a lot of time in the dark shed part of his run. We were warned that Mo did not like men and that my husband was to keep his distance. I entered the enclosure area at the back of Mo's shed that was separated from the enclosure by wire. This was an area for people to greet him, well women away. He presented me with his back to scratch. Each time I stopped scratching him and turned to speak to the lady that was with us, Mo would climb across the wire wall holding on to it and quietly place his back under the palm of my hand, as his cue he needed another scratch.

Then suddenly Mo went mad. He had caught a glimpse of my husband watching our interaction from around the corner. My husband quickly moved away and out of sight. Mo immediately calmed and continued to move himself to ask for his scratch again. Just the visual sight of a man caused his past association of 'men equal fear and harm', had come into play. My husband was still as close, so it was not Mo's olfactory system that was picking up on him in his environment. It was purely a visual observation

of a man and association of what men meant to him that caused his reaction.

We can also see psychological safety zone behaviour in many other species and especially I horses: The ex-race horse that shakes at the mere thought of leaving the confinement of his stable and is unable to deal with the vastness of the green field. Not to mention those humans that have spent years cooped up in their home, barely leaving as they have been unable to deal with the outside world.

On reflection it is easy to put all of these instances into the same box. What is often failed to be seen and is so important is that, although these situations may appear to present with the same symptoms. Not all of these situations are in fact the same, regardless of following a pattern.

For some horses and people it is fear of not being able to control the fear once it is felt, that is what has caused the snowball effect. It is not necessarily the fear of the outside that is foundational to the issue. But rather, that once they are outside of their comfort zone and physically outside. Should the fear manifest, can they actually get back 'physically' and therefore 'mentally' to their comfort zone? The fear of not being able to, and fearing the fear may manifest, can be enough for some to want to remain to a large degree self-imprisoned. What may be seen as a fear of outside and large environment, may in fact be fear by association of fear and not actually fear of anything physical other than the feeling itself.

The understanding of the true cause of such behaviour through communication is power-mount in understanding how to help the horse over-come their fear. Is it even in their best interests to even over-come it? As I feel it is safe to say that in some cases, what we may see as the journey to healing for that individual, can in fact be psychologically breaking and a closing down of the psychological emotional state and 'self' - as a coping mechanism. When this happens the fear has not really gone - it is just hidden. The healing has not really been created and what we have created in our arrogance in wanting to heal another in the wrong way, or through our naivety, is a psychologically broken closed down mind. One that appears and presents outwardly and physically as healed and in acceptance, is sadly often very far from the truth. All we may have created due to our lack of understand of the psychology of the individual, is a need for them to create a coping mechanism.

It is for this reason that unless we have an indepth knowledge of psychology and behaviour, we have to seriously consider if these are the kind of communications that we should be engaging in at all. By not having the correct knowledge in place, we could lead others to cause more harm than good, at great cost to the mind of the horse involved.

However, when our understanding of psychology and behaviour is in place and the analytical mind is at play and is able to see all sides of the coin. (Not just heads and tails, but also inside and not forgetting the outer circle that holds it all together). Then we may be in a situation where the horse and their Guardian could greatly benefit from our insight, aside from the communication. Not only this, but if we do not have the knowledge in place. Then we fall prey to hearing, but not actually understanding, what is being said to us by the horse. As so often it is not what they say - but what they mean. Those two important things do not always tally in a way that makes sense.

Words can be empty and can only be of use if the one hearing them understands beyond them. A horse (and indeed a person) that does not fully understand their own psychology, is not fully able to make you understand from their point of view. As the individual is unable to put how they feel into words in the depth that they need to. Therefore it is our role, should we be knowledgeable enough to work with it, to 'know' the story and psychology behind those words. If we do not, my advice is to steer clear and leave such communications to those that do have the knowledge needed. As the last thing we want to do is cause the horse pain, by interpreting incorrectly and advising wrongly based on our own lack of knowledge and experience. Our role is to help and aid, not hinder and cause anguish to the already fragile mind and where and how it chooses to keep itself safe and free of collapse.

# SAVE THEM ALL SYNDROME

This is the term I use for those that feel the need to save 'everything' - by everything I am meaning both animals and people.

Those that scream to stop eating meat - close the slaughterhouses and stop slave labour. Not for one minute am I saying that I don't want those things to be stopped. They serve no true purpose in the grand scheme of things - or within our evolution. They are cruel, they are barbaric, and those that engage in such activities are not truth seekers or the compassionate - they are the greedy. As greedy if not more so, than those that choose to buy, consume and use their products, those that enable the plight to continue. The same consumers that so often are those that are screaming for these things to come to an end and be made illegal.

*Now I will draw breathe before I write the next part. Please read carefully before making judgment.*

*If we ban factory farming tomorrow and close the slaughterhouses, what will happen to those animals already in existence?*

*Where will they live?*

*Who will feed them and pay for their food?*

*Who will pay for their veterinary care?*

*Will the farmers buy food and turn them out into lovely fields and go and stack shelves in a supermarket to pay for it all?*

*Will the Vets work for the rest of their lives for free, even taking on a second job to pay for the drugs they need?*

*Will YOU home, feed and get medical care for all of these millions of animals and people?*

*Provide those people with housing, food, medical care and nurture and raise the children who have lost parents in factory fires and through starvation?*

*If we ban factory farming right now – today - will there be enough crops already in place to feed the worlds human and animal populations, or will they face large scale starvation?*

*If we ban the low paid factories in China, how will those people feed themselves?*

*How will they find new work and income?*

*Who is going to fed, pay and care for all of the horses, cats and dogs as well as other species that are in kill shelters. Should euthanasia due to lack of a home become illegal?*

*Are you going to pay for it all?*
*I guess not....so how can we change it other than through education over overbreeding ?*

The sad truth is that humans have created a big fat mess within our world. They have caused havoc, suffering and eventually collapse should it continue.

Rather than instantly banning everything and throwing the world into even more chaos. We need to look at the foundational issues. Look to how we can create change and end the suffering long term, in such a way as we do not create more in doing so.

*How can we create good pay for those working in slave labour?*

*How can we provide a world-wide alternative to meat consumption that is both humane and long term?*

*If we do this how we can we prevent species from becoming extinct?*

*How can we educate people without force to consider what is on their plate and how it got there?*

*How can we offer support in creating those changes?*

*How can we do it without judgment and the patronising of individuals?*

*How can we aid and not force them into wanting to create change, both for themselves and for others on a large scale?*

Telling someone they are selfish is not going to cut it. Telling people they are wrong without being able to back up your reasoning is not going to swing it either. People need to work it out for themselves. They need to be supported when they feel the time for inner self exploration of themselves is needed - at the right time that it is needed and when they are ready.

As long as people fear and withdraw from waking up - change will not come. Be the person you are and can be, be the real you and lead by example. Until you are able to do this it is unfair and unjust to criticise another.

So often it is just the meeting of another individual that can cause the inspiration of some and help them to see more clearly. As in the story of Claire and Bella in my book - 'From their heart to yours - Inspirational horses and the people who love them'.

It is lunch time as I sit here typing this, an average day of inspiration and smiles. Tears today also but good ones. This has come about due to receiving three messages from people who feel that I have inspired them into looking to create change within themselves and in what they do. Enabling them to find how they also choose to reflect that outwardly to the world as they find their true selves. That is part of my role and in some ways helping others truly find themselves and how they choose to reflect that, is my own selfish way in which fulfilment comes to me also. It creates change all round for the greater good.

There is also another element to 'Save Them All Syndrome'. That is often the role of many Animal Communicators and Healers. Often the reason that we have taken on the role as Communicators and Healers, is due to our love and compassion for animals. It is only natural to want to provide a stress free and pain free life for not only those we consider our own, but also all others. Where ever they may be in the world and what-ever their circumstances.

Let's take a step back from this a moment and put it into perspective.

*Why are they there?*

*The horse not being fed correctly, or not given enough food; why is he choosing to stay?*

The horse enclosed within the paddock fencing: one that can easy jump and leave if he so chooses to. Chances are it is within his life path to be there, or he may not know anything else is out there to leave for and to. Maybe he has been institutionalised and learnt helplessness has crept in over the years. Then again....maybe quite simply it is just his choice and that for whatever reason he chooses therefore to stay.

Whatever the reason in the grand scheme of things, it is 'their' path. A reason that is valid to them and it is not for us to rush into 'every' situation and try and change it. Where that horse is, may at that moment be exactly where they need to be, in order to learn and grow in their own way. If we rush in and create uninvited change in every situation that is not to our own liking, we are taking away choice from another.

We can't 'heal all', not all are meant or want to be healed. Wading in with our idealistic view of how we think another should have to live and what they should have to experience, is neither constructive to their life, or our own integrity within our work.

Nor is it constructive or kind to prolong a physical existence, when it is time to shed the outer body that is in pain and the individual's time is up. 'A short life that has been fulfilled is better than a long one empty', is my motto. Therefore when the right time has come to pass, how can we in our loving and understanding nature choose to try and override that? To inflict suffering through the forced staying of that individual that needs to go? Why instead are we not standing by their side loving them - supporting them when they need to pass in the best way we can? Instead of standing selfishly crying for ourselves and 'our' perceived 'loss'?

Instead we must choose to respect what help, or lack of help each horse feels willing and able to accept, as well as the way in which they need it. It is then our role to create that offering for them, to use in such a way as they feel best for themselves. Best put, step back and let others create their own decisions as to their own welfare and how they choose to live, so long as it is not harming others. They may not yet be ready to understand in the way you do, and with the perception you have, that enables you to see all possibilities. Instead stand back, support them as best you can and extend the hand of offering and friendship to them. In such a way that they know you are aiding them in their working their way towards their true self and where they need to be right now. If they need you, they will ask you - offer do not inflict.

Around four years ago I was very ill, I had lost so much weight that I was only registering at six stone. I was weak, having dizzy spells and could barely drag myself out of bed, let alone feed myself. Yet all of this time my animals were fed and cared for, their needs met. However, as a realist I was also aware that it was only a matter of time before I would be unable to care for my horses and what that physically involved. I had recently almost passed out in a field of snow pushing a wheel barrow at 11pm one night, in a bid to get soaked hay out to my horses, so one of them would not cough. Having already bucketed the twenty buckets of water out of the bath and carried it outside as needed to soak the hay. I had to think sensibility for their sakes.

I put my property up for sale and re-homed one of my horses with a good friend. When I left him there I cried all the way home out of worry for him, even though I knew he was in safe hands. My husband pulled the car over and told me he could turn around, that we could go back and get him - I told him to keep driving. My friend bless her, told me she was not changing his passport and putting it into her name. That when the day came that I felt well enough he would still be there waiting for me. I honestly believed that day would never come and told her as much. It was the end of the road, he was hers now.

Seven weeks passed and I could barely sleep. I was worse, but I was also aware I was worse because I did not have Alfi with me. Late one night I called my friend telling her desperately that both Alfi and I needed him to come home. She replied that that was fine; she knew it would happen she just did not expect it so soon!

The following weekend we drove to collect him. From day one he had attracted a new friend whilst he was at my friend's yard. A little black Arabian named Manta. A some-what confused and odd but very loveable individual - visually beautiful and inwardly even more so. Part of me felt guilty that they were having to part company - but the future as later played out was to change all of that.

Alfi arrived home and settled instantly back with his two little pony friends. Manta was never far from my mind and it was not unusual when not thinking of him for the picture of his face to come to mind, as if he was saying 'do not forget about me'.

Time passed and sadly it was time to bid a fond farewell to one of our little pony friends Meeka. She had developed a brain tumour and neurological issues had started to appear. Now there was just Alfi and his little friend Cinders. A little pony that sadly was not in the best of health - partly due to poor breeding and the greed of humans. Cinders was happy for now but she was living on borrowed time, any month could have been her last. It was time to go in search for an additional friend for Alfi and I.

I called my friend and dropped the relevant hints needed about a certain little black Arabian in her care. About a month later on a wet gusty fowl weathered day Manta was loaded onto a trailer and arrived back at Nirvana Springs.

Manta 'called' as he stepped off the trailer, he was out of view and yet his voice was enough to cause Alfi to recognise him and prick his ears at the all familiar call. As Manta did his impressive extended trot around the summer paddock in order to assess its boundaries and all they included Alfi followed, a somewhat confused expression upon his face.

Needless to say that was a few years ago now. Little Cinders has since made her way to the great beyond for the next part of her journey and Alfi and Manta still live happily side by side. Along with a new addition - Alfi's half brother, another in need named Harree, yet again a twist of destiny that I had never set out looking for. Through circumstances playing out in the right way, he was aided in finding his way home to us.

# LOOKING GLASS SYNDROME

'Looking Glass Syndrome' is a term I use to explain our perception. The following is a metaphor that I use in order to explain further:

Imagine a dark land - on the land sits a house full of all of the world's different species. The house has many different windows, each with their own unique differences. Some of the windows will be clear and have beautiful views. Some will only show darkness. Some have frosted glass that causes distortion, and some allow you to see nothing at all. There will also be those that show the view of faraway lands, mapping the horizon and allow for the playing out of scenes that we are able to observe and understand. Each one of these scenes will be different; some nice and some not so. Each window and what it has to offer is different for each individual that chooses to stand and stare.

Those in the house will find the window that suits them; the one that enables them to feel the most comfortable. Some may even choose to spend their whole life in that one position, just staring and never venturing to explore or even consider another view. In fact, they may be so static that they are not even aware that another view and another perspective is even possible and exists.

Over time some will choose to move and explore. They will go to the windows of others, enabling them to see not just in their own way, but also as others do. Some may choose to do this only once in their life time, whilst others will make it their role in life to continuously see all points of view - all windows, enabling them to learn and develop further.

Then we find the Truth Seeker; the one who has had enough of windows, views and the perceptions of both themselves and others. They believe there to be more to life and they go in search of it. Some may spend years walking around inside the house, only to come across more perceptions - more views. Only one day to find the door that leads them to the great outside. Some may be tentative, even concerned about going outside. Some may stand and wait a while until such a time as they feel ready. Others may grab the door knob and scream 'Thank goodness as I knew there was more to it!'.

When the time is right they will step outside. It may seem dark at first as only too often the distorted or perfectionist view of the windows are incorrect - as seen by those that have ventured outside. As realisation comes and the dark mists start to clear, the veil lifts and truth is now truly observed. No longer is that individual clouded, pulled down and distorted by the vision of others. They now have found the truth in what they seek and are able to see as is truly meant. They close their eyes and give acknowledgment and thanks. They then tip back their head as they open their eyes and they see the sky. 'WOW....this is only the very beginning of the awakening'.

The truth is that not all individuals have the strength of mind to venture outside and some may just be happy within their own perception and their 'lot'. It does not make them bad individuals, nor does it make them stupid. It is just where they are on their life path and within their fragile psyche. It will be dependent on life lessons that they have chosen to reject or to take on board willingly, and what their early experiences have both offered and denied them.

The meat eater that declares he loves eating meat will likely never make it out of the house. He will likely never reach the window that offers the slaughterhouse scene. Those that are unable to cope with the death of a loved one will likely never see the sight of the funeral directors back room - they will choose not to venture to that window.

However, when we choose to explore all elevations and all windows, we are able to acknowledge each for what they are. We can do so without having to close our eyes to misery and the plight of others due to an inability to cope with our own emotions. Instead, we will be able to understand how they feel, why they think the way they do, and we will be able to find some kind of peace within it. Knowing that is them, we do not need to be like them if we do not choose to be. We can find another perspective and choose to look through the clear windows and then look to the skies for the answers.

No two individuals will be the same; how can they be? Each of their life paths will have offered different life lessons, different circumstances and events. Each of these will have offered them a way to move forwards and even the option to hold back.

The psyche can be fragile; some are already broken beyond repair as shown by our psychiatric words and the sadly disturbed individuals they home, and those that choose to hide in their houses, stable or kennel as the outside world is just too over whelming. Often these are the ones that chose to venture outside too quickly, enabling them to explore too many windows and perceptions first. As well as those forced out with little understanding of others and how and why they do the things that they do to each other - the agoraphobic racing horse; to the abused child and the dog used as bait for fighting dogs.

However, there will be those that know that whatever life has thrown at them - does not have to shape them. They understand that they are not their circumstances or their experiences, but that innately there is more. These are the survivors in life, the ones that choose to heal and can heal to varying degrees by facing their fears, their challenges ahead and wanting to overcome the uncomfortable feeling that exists in the moment. They do this in the full knowledge that life in its entirety is waiting for them. Those individuals are those that I hold the most respect for, those that have found the inner strength to throw caution to the wind. Those that feel the fear and do it anyway. These are the warriors of life that will help to bring through a whole new generation of believers in 'self'.

This does not mean for one moment I hold any form of disrespect whatsoever for those that have not ventured outside. Rather, I see where they are in their life and in their own minds, as where they need to be and within their copying of life. But as a truth seeker and having known the journey to get here, I know the struggles and what it entails. Any that choose to tread that path have my greatest respect and support.

# SYMPATHY VS EMPATHY

How we choose to work and how we think will have a huge impact on our emotional state when we are working with horses. Also, how we view them and how we cope with their illnesses and 'passings', as well as our emotional issues surrounding them.

Simply put: when we choose to work with sympathy, we leave ourselves open to be dragged into another's drama. We allow our own emotions to be affected by those of others. We finish our work, leave the company of that horse or person and we feel awful. We feel sad for their pain and we are worried about them. We can even have trouble sleeping through having them 'on our mind'. Whilst there is nothing wrong with sympathy in as much as it shows only too well the level of compassion innate to us. It does not serve us, and nor is it positive for our own emotional health. It does not help the horses and people that may need our help and support and need us to be fully focused and present when we are in their company. If we are left worrying about a horse, that will be on our mind and our focus is not fully directed in the area that it needs to be when we are in the company of others. There are even instances when some horses and people may even feel patronised by another's sympathy towards them.

However, when we choose to work with empathy - this enables us to understand how the horse feels. At the same time it enables us to be able to safely guide our own emotions in such a way that we do not take the horse's negativity, or sorrow upon ourselves. This enables us to support the individual with a positive outlook and approach, enabling us to help and inspire, as well as seeing the positive within a negative experience. It will stop us from being drained by their personal drama. By drama I am not insinuating in a patronising manner that they are creating drama. But rather, through circumstance, drama has manifested, not necessarily instigated by them and which may be beyond their control.

Empathy is supporting and creating an ideal that lacks and holds no agenda in changing another's life path, or interfering with it. It is the art of being able to play the observer; to watch, hear and understand what is playing out - without becoming directly involved. Working with empathy as the observer also enables us to stand back and see the bigger picture, rather than being directly emotionally involved. It aids us in being able to see things are they truly are and objectively. It enables us to view through the distortion of emotions, removing biased approach and outcome and gets us right to the heart of the matter.

When we let go of ego and we are able to step back without the need to be overly involved emotionally. We are able to deal with much needed matters at hand in a calm and constructive way. This may be emergency restraining of a horse for their own safety in the case of serious injury, to the ability to stand with a horse as he passes, without crying or bombarding him with any form of negative emotion on our part. Due to how we may otherwise be feeling.

In instances such as these, we are then able to keep our head, keep our breath and heart rate low, and safely manage our own energy. This will benefit the horse in question no end, because it is coming from a place of empathy rather than a state of just not caring. It will carry the correct vibration, feel authentic and be of no end of benefit to the horse, enabling them the opportunity to synchronise with our own brain wave state and other physiological functions that will further aid them in maintaining their own calmness in how they deal with their presenting situation.

Imagine a bubble around each individual; each bubble being the energy of their emotions. When we choose to allow that bubble to come into contact with our own and we invade another's emotional energy, it mixes with our own – this is sympathy. We then enable it to distort our own emotional state. The art of empathy however, is when we choose to stand back and observe and read the energy of emotions. We can then see them with clarity. Our own emotional state is intact and we are not distorting the energy of emotions for another individual with our own, should a negative mind-set prevail within us at any given time.

So for the sake of yourself and the horse whose company you are in, please choose to work with empathy over sympathy. They will thank you for it.

I feel it is also important to point out sentience within our empathy, and how this can cause us to still feel the horse's emotions when we are in the company of a horse. In the same way that they are affected by us through our breath rate, brain wave state and other biological functions. We too will be affected by theirs and this can in many cases cause a change in our own mental and emotional state. This is very different from sympathy and does not automatically mean that it is sympathy that we are experiencing. Rather, this is just a normal physical reaction to the environment that we have found ourselves in. If we are working with empathy, then when we remove ourselves from the company of the horse, our body will physically change back to how it was before, as it is no longer synchronising with the biological functions of the horse that is feeling emotionally uncomfortable.

# ABOUT THE AUTHOR

Holly has been working as a professional Animal Communicator since 1999. She currently lives in Wales with her seven cats and three Arabian horses.

She is the Author of many books and courses on animal therapies. These are available throughout the UK as well as Internationally.

She has a keen interest in natural behaviour and medicine as well as, psychological disorders in animals and Neuroscience. A huge amount of her time is spent helping people to understand their animals, aid in their recovery, and create a better life for them.

Holly was one of the first Animal Communicators to teach workshops in UK and is the Author of the first recognised Animal Communication Diploma in the UK.

Her accredited courses are available through Stonebridge College. Links for which can be found on her website.

### www.hollydavis.co.uk

Holly's Animal Healing Workshop CD is also available through her website. This CD is highly recommended for those who wish to learn Animal Communication. As it contains guided instructions to follow to enable you to make a connection with animals.

## Other books in the series:

Myth Magic and Mayhem

The Revelations

Healing for Horses

More available soon, please visit website for details.

Printed in Great Britain
by Amazon.co.uk, Ltd.,
Marston Gate.